Developing Core Literacy Proficiencies

GRADE 6

Student Edition

GRADE
6

STUDENT EDITION

Developing
Core Literacy
Proficiencies

ODELL
EDUCATION

JB JOSSEY-BASS™
A Wiley Brand

Published by Jossey-Bass

A Wiley Brand

One Montgomery Street, Suite 1000, San Francisco, CA 94104–4594—www.josseybass.com

Jossey-Bass books and products are available through most bookstores. To contact Jossey-Bass directly call our Customer Care Department within the U.S. at 800–956–7739, outside the U.S. at 317–572–3986, or fax 317–572–4002.

Wiley publishes in a variety of print and electronic formats and by print-on-demand. Some material included with standard print versions of this book may not be included in e-books or in print-on-demand. If this book refers to media such as a CD or DVD that is not included in the version you purchased, you may download this material at www.wiley.com/go/coreliteracy (use the following password: odell2016). For more information about Wiley products, visit www.wiley.com.

Library of Congress Cataloging-in-Publication Data

Names: Odell Education, author.
Title: Developing core literacy proficiencies. Grade 6 / Odell Education.
Description: Student edition. | San Francisco, CA : Jossey-Bass, 2016.
Identifiers: LCCN 2016002271 (print) | LCCN 2016012614 (ebook) |
  ISBN 9781119192787 (paperback) | ISBN 9781119192800 (pdf) | ISBN 9781119192794 (epub)
Subjects: LCSH: Language arts (Elementary)—Curricula—United States. |
  Common Core State Standards (Education)
Classification: LCC LB1576 .O344 2016b (print) | LCC LB1576 (ebook) | DDC
  372.6—dc23
LC record available at http://lccn.loc.gov/2016002271

Cover Design: Wiley
Cover Image: ©Danae Olaso/EyeEm/Getty Images, Inc.

Printed in the United States of America

FIRST EDITION

PB Printing   10 9 8 7 6 5 4 3 2 1

ACKNOWLEDGMENTS

Project director: Stephanie Smythe

Primary program designers:

- Rick Dills, EdD
- Judson Odell
- Ioana Radoi
- Daniel Fennessy

Curriculum consultant: Nemeesha Brown

Contributing text specialist: Rosemarie Heinegg, PhD

Unit developers—Texts, notes, and questions:

- Reading Closely for Textual Details: "The wolf you feed": Rick Dills, EdD
- Making Evidence-Based Claims: "Connecting the Dots": Rick Dills, EdD
- Researching to Deepen Understanding: "Prehistoric Cave Art": Rosemarie Heinegg, PhD, and Luke Bauer
- Building Evidence-Based Arguments: "Energy Crossroads": Daniel Fennessy and Rick Dills, EdD

We are grateful for feedback we received on early versions of units from Achieve's EQuIP Review Process, under the direction of Christine Tell, Alissa Peltzman, and Cristina Marks.

We are also grateful for the students and teachers of the Bay Shore Schools who collaborated with us to pilot the curriculum. Thanks especially to LaQuita Outlaw, Elizabeth Galarza, Caitlin Moreira, and Jen Ritter (who personally renamed the Supporting Evidence-Based Claims Tool).

We are especially grateful for New York State and the Regents Research Fund for funding the development of the earlier Open Educational Resource version of this curriculum. Without the support we received from Kristen Huff, David Abel, and Kate Gerson, none of this work would have been possible.

CONTENTS

All materials from the Literacy Toolbox are available as editable and printable PDFs at
www.wiley.com/go/coreliteracy. Use the following password: odell2016.

INTRODUCTION TO THE CORE LITERACY PROFICIENCIES: BECOMING A LITERATE PERSON

"Literacy is the ability to use printed and written information to function in society, to achieve one's goals, and to develop one's knowledge and potential."

—Definition from the National
Assessment of Adult Literacy

Becoming a Literate Person: Your school and teachers are trying to help you succeed in life—and to be the best you can be at whatever you choose to do. One of the ways they are doing this is by developing your *literacy*—but what do we mean when we talk about your literacy? A dictionary might simply tell us that developing literacy means building your *skills* as a reader, thinker, and writer—but it also might tell us that literacy is *knowledge* in an area of learning that is important to you. In addition, being literate involves ways of thinking and doing things—*habits*—that a person develops over time.

Being a literate person is even more important today—in our computer-driven world—than it was in the past, no matter what you want to do:

- Go to college and become a scientist
- Be a designer, artist, musician, or chef
- Own your own business
- Develop computer applications or video games
- Work in an industry or a construction field
- Seek a career in the military
- Just want to keep up with the news of the world

You will need to be literate whatever path in school and life you choose to follow. A recent study of the reading challenges faced by people in the United States found out that the textbooks students see in their first two years of college are much more challenging than the ones they use in high school—one reason so many new college students struggle. But the study also found that technical manuals, informational websites, and even newspapers demand a high level of reading and thinking skills as well as specialized knowledge and strategic habits—they demand literacy.

Core Literacy Proficiencies: The learning experiences you will discover in the Odell Education Program are designed to help you take control of your own literacy development and build the skills, knowledge, and habits you will need to be successful in life. They are also designed to excite your imagination and engage you in activities that are interesting and challenging.

The learning activities you will encounter will help you develop four key Core Literacy Proficiencies. What do we mean by this term? We've already discussed the importance of *literacy*. *Core* suggests that what you will be learning is at the center—of your literacy development, your overall success in school, and your future life. The word *proficiency* is also important, because being "proficient" at something means you can do it well, can do it on your own, and have the confidence that comes with being good at something. Developing proficiency takes time, practice, and determination. However, becoming proficient is one of the great rewards of learning—whether you are learning to read closely, to play a musical instrument, or to do a difficult skateboard trick.

Literacy Proficiency Units: The Core Literacy Proficiencies you will develop in each of four units are as follows:

1. *Reading Closely for Textual Details:* In this unit you will develop your proficiency as an

investigator of texts. You will learn how to do the following:

- Examine things closely (images, videos, websites, and texts)
- Ask and use questions to guide your close examination
- Find the key details—clues—that tell you something
- Make connections among those details
- Use those connections to develop an observation or conclusion

2. *Making Evidence-Based Claims:* In this unit you will develop your proficiency as a *maker and prover of claims.* You will learn how to do the following:

- Use the details, connections, and evidence you find in a text to form a claim—a stated conclusion—about something you have discovered
- Organize evidence from the text to support your claim and make your case
- Express and explain your claim in writing
- Improve your writing so that others will clearly understand and appreciate your evidence-based claim—and think about the case you have made for it

3. *Researching to Deepen Understanding:* In this unit you will develop your proficiency as a *finder and user of information.* You will learn how to do the following:

- Have an inquiring mind and ask good questions
- Search for information—in texts, interviews, and on the Internet—that can help you answer your questions
- Record and organize the information you find
- Decide what is relevant and trustworthy in the sources of your information
- Come to a research-based position or solution to a problem
- Clearly communicate what you have learned

4. *Building Evidence-Based Arguments:* In this unit you will develop your proficiency as a *presenter of reasoned arguments.* You will learn how to do the following:

- Understand the background and key aspects of an important issue
- Look at various viewpoints on the issue
- Read the arguments of others closely and thoughtfully
- Develop your own view of the issue and take a stand about it
- Make and prove your case by using sound evidence and reasoning to support it
- Improve your writing so that others will clearly understand and appreciate your evidence-based argument—and think about the case you have made for it

Materials to Develop Literacy Proficiency: In each of the units, you will use the supporting materials organized in this Student Edition:

Texts   Each unit includes a set of relatively short but challenging texts, which you will read, examine, and discuss.

Tools   Each unit has its own *toolbox*—a set of graphic organizers that help you think about what you are reading or writing and record your thinking so you can discuss it with others and come back to it later.

Handouts   Each unit has a set of handouts, some of which will help you understand important things you are learning and some of which will help you be successful in completing the assignments in the unit.

Literacy Skills and Academic Habits
Throughout the units you will be developing Literacy Skills and Academic Habits. You will use these skills and habits to monitor your own growth and give feedback to other students when reading, discussing, and writing. Your teacher may use them to let you know about your areas of strength and areas in which you need to improve.

Introduction to the Core Literacy Proficiencies

LITERACY SKILLS	DESCRIPTORS
ATTENDING TO DETAILS	Identifies words, details, or quotations that are important to understanding the text
DECIPHERING WORDS	Uses context and vocabulary to define unknown words and phrases
COMPREHENDING SYNTAX	Recognizes and uses sentence structures to help understand the text
INTERPRETING LANGUAGE	Understands how words are used to express ideas and perspectives
IDENTIFYING RELATIONSHIPS	Notices important connections among details, ideas, or texts
MAKING INFERENCES	Draws sound conclusions from reading and examining the text closely
SUMMARIZING	Correctly explains what the text says about the topic
QUESTIONING	Writes questions that help identify important ideas, connections, and perspectives in a text
RECOGNIZING PERSPECTIVE	Identifies and explains the author's view of the text's topic
EVALUATING INFORMATION	Assesses the relevance and credibility of information in texts
DELINEATING ARGUMENTATION	Identifies and analyzes the claims, evidence, and reasoning in arguments
FORMING CLAIMS	States a meaningful conclusion that is well supported by evidence from the text
USING EVIDENCE	Uses well-chosen details from the text to support explanations; accurately paraphrases or quotes
USING LOGIC	Supports a position through a logical sequence of related claims, premises, and supporting evidence
USING LANGUAGE	Writes and speaks clearly so others can understand claims and ideas
PRESENTING DETAILS	Inserts details and quotations effectively into written or spoken explanations
ORGANIZING IDEAS	Organizes claims, supporting ideas, and evidence in a logical order
USING CONVENTIONS	Correctly uses sentence elements, punctuation, and spelling to produce clear writing
PUBLISHING	Correctly uses, formats, and cites textual evidence to support claims
REFLECTING CRITICALLY	Uses literacy concepts to discuss and evaluate personal and peer learning

ACADEMIC HABITS	DESCRIPTORS
PREPARING	Reads the text(s) closely and thinks about the questions to prepare for tasks
ENGAGING ACTIVELY	Focuses attention on the task when working individually and with others
COLLABORATING	Works well with others while participating in text-centered discussions and group activities
COMMUNICATING CLEARLY	Presents ideas and supporting evidence so others can understand them
LISTENING	Pays attention to ideas from others and takes time to think about them
GENERATING IDEAS	Generates and develops ideas, positions, products, and solutions to problems
ORGANIZING WORK	Maintains materials so that they can be used effectively and efficiently
COMPLETING TASKS	Finishes short and extended tasks by established deadlines
REVISING	Rethinks ideas and refines work based on feedback from others
UNDERSTANDING PURPOSE AND PROCESS	Understands why and how a task should be accomplished
REMAINING OPEN	Asks questions of others rather than arguing for a personal idea or opinion
QUALIFYING VIEWS	Modifies and further justifies ideas in response to thinking from others

READING CLOSELY
FOR TEXTUAL DETAILS

DEVELOPING CORE LITERACY
PROFICIENCIES

GRADE 6

"The wolf you feed"

GOAL

In this unit you will develop your proficiency as an investigator of texts. You will learn how to do the following:

1. Examine things closely (images, videos, websites, and texts).
2. Ask and use questions to guide your close examination.
3. Find the key details—clues—that tell you something.
4. Make connections among those details.
5. Use those connections to develop an observation or conclusion.

TOPIC

In this unit—titled "The wolf you feed" (a quote from an Indian legend)—you will be learning about the ways humans have viewed the wolf over time and what we now know and think about the hunting and social behavior of wolves. You will study some fascinating pictures of wolves, watch a video, explore websites, and read short informational texts and a story that present various views of wolves.

ACTIVITIES

You will start by examining a set of photos and graphic images to develop your skills of looking closely for key details, then work on these same skills with a video and websites. When you read, the details you look for will be things such as key information or statistics, explanations, and pictures the author creates through images and sentences. You'll also look for important words that you need to understand because they tell you something about the topic and how the author views it. You will learn how to use questions the way an expert investigator does—in this case to dig deeply into what you are seeing or reading. Those questions will also guide the discussions you will have with other students and your teacher. From your investigation of the texts, you will come to your own understanding of the topic of wolves and their behavior—which you will then share with others through a final written explanation and a discussion you will lead.

READING CLOSELY FOR TEXTUAL DETAILS LITERACY TOOLBOX

In *Reading Closely for Textual Details*, you will begin to build your "literacy toolbox" by learning how to use the following handouts, tools and checklists organized in your Student Edition.

Developing Core Literacy Proficiencies

TOOLS

To support your work with the texts, you will learn how to use the following tools:

Approaching the Text Tool

This two-part tool helps you prepare to read a text closely. It provides places to think about what you initially know about the text as you *approach* it—your purpose for reading, the author, publication date, and so on. It also lets you record several *questions* that you can use to do a first reading and then a rereading of the text.

Analyzing Details Tool

This four-part tool supports you in developing and using the key skills of the unit: searching for and *selecting* key details or quotations, *recording* references from the text about where you found the details and quotations, *analyzing* what those details mean to you as a reader, and *connecting* the details to form your understanding of the text.

Questioning Path Tool

This graphic organizer will provide places for you to record questions you or your teacher want to think about as you read a particular text. You will be able to record general Guiding Questions and also questions that are very specific to the text you are reading. What you record in the **Questioning Path Tool** can help you initially *approach* the text, *question* it during a first reading and investigation, *analyze* it further, *deepen* your understanding, and *extend* your reading and thinking to other questions and texts.

Model Questioning Paths

For each text you will read, there is a **Questioning Path Tool** that has been filled out for you to frame and guide your reading. These model Questioning Paths are just starting points, and your teacher or you may prefer to develop your own paths. The model paths are organized by the steps from the **Reading Closely Graphic** (*approaching, questioning, analyzing, deepening,* and *extending*) and include general Guiding Questions from the Guiding Questions Handout and some questions that are specific to each text and its content. You will use these model paths to guide your reading, frame your discussions with your teacher and other students, and help you when you are doing the final activities in the unit.

HANDOUTS

To support your work with the texts and the tools, you will be able to use the following informational handouts:

Reading Closely Graphic

This graphic helps you understand the relationship among the various steps you will follow as you use questions to read a text closely: *approaching, questioning, analyzing, deepening,* and *extending.*

Guiding Questions Handout

This handout organizes a set of good, general questions to use when you are reading any text—called *Guiding Questions*. The questions are organized in rows that match the questioning process in the **Reading Closely Graphic** (*approaching, questioning, analyzing, deepening,* and *extending*) and also by four areas that we often pay attention to when we read a text.

Attending to Details Handout

This handout presents descriptions and examples of the kinds of details you might look for as you read a text, for example, facts and statistics, explanations of things, images and word pictures, technical terms, and so on.

Text-Based Explanation—Final Writing and Discussion Assignment

This handout will explain to you what you will be doing in the two-part final assignment for this unit: (1) writing a multiparagraph explanation of an understanding you have come to about the topic and one of the texts and (2) participating in and leading a discussion of your text and how it compares to others in the unit. The handout will also help you know what your teacher will be looking for so you can be successful on the assignments.

 # CHECKLISTS

You will also use this checklist throughout the unit to support peer- and self-review:

Reading Closely Skills and Habits Checklist

This checklist presents and briefly describes the Literacy Skills and Habits you will be working on during the unit. You can use it to remind you of what you are trying to learn. You can also use it to reflect on what you have done when reading, discussing, or writing. It can help you give feedback to other students. Your teacher may use it to let you know about your areas of strength and areas in which you need to improve.

READING CLOSELY FOR TEXTUAL DETAILS UNIT TEXTS

AUTHOR	DATE	PUBLISHER	NOTES
Text 1: Representations of Wolves (Images)			
Various	NA	Various: public domain	Wolves represented through art, illustration, and photography
Text 2: "A Brief History of Wolves in the United States" (Informational text)			
Cornelia N. Hutt	NA	*Kids Planet*	Overview of wolves in North America including how they have been seen and affected by various groups of humans
Text 3: *Two Wolves* (Video)			
Dave Owens	2008	Dave Owens	A Cherokee story of wisdom; the words of a Cherokee grandfather talking to his grandson
Text 4: *Living with Wolves* and *Lobos of the South West* (Websites)			
NA	NA	Living with Wolves and Mexican Wolves.org	Informational websites about wolves—one on the history of the Mexican gray wolf and one about wolves living on a preserve
Text 5: "All About Wolves": Hunting Behavior (Informational text)			
John Vucetich and Rolf Peterson	2012	The Wolves and Moose of Isle Royale Project	An overview of the Isle Royale Project as well as a factual description of a wolf hunt
Text 6: *White Fang.*(Pt. II, Ch. I) (Fictional narrative)			
Jack London	1906	Macmillan	Excerpt focusing on the running of a wolf pack and the role of the dominant female wolf within the pack
Text 7: "All About Wolves": Pack Behavior (Informational text)			
John Vucetich and Rolf Peterson	2012	The Wolves and Moose of Isle Royale Project	Discussion of the social behavior of wolves
Text 8: *White Fang.* (Pt. II, Ch. III) (Fictional narrative)			
Jack London	1906	Macmillan	Excerpt describing the first sensory experiences of a wolf pup and the role of the wolf parents

Text 9: "We Didn't Domesticate Dogs. They Domesticated Us." (Scientific study)			
Brian Hare and Vanessa Woods	2013	*National Geographic*	An article exploring why and how wolves and humans commenced an enduring and, eventually, affectionate relationship
Extended reading: Extension texts exploring various aspects of wolves and human perception of them.			
Extended reading: "Why Wolves Are Forever Wild and Dogs Can Be Tamed"			
Jennifer Viegas	2013	*Discovery News*	An accessible article explaining how the difference between wolves and dogs begins at birth
Extended Reading: "Dogs, but Not Wolves, Use Humans as Tools"			
Jason G. Goldman	2012	*Scientific American* blog	A more complex article that details an experiment to see whether dogs' relationships with humans are driven by genetic or experiential factors
Extended Reading: "How Werewolves Work"			
Tracy V. Wilson	N/A	How Stuff Works	An article that explores the historical and cultural origins of the concept of the werewolf
Extended Reading: Interview with Suzanne Stone			
Suzanne Asha Stone	2009	Idaho Public Television	An interview with the director of wolf conservation programs in Idaho, Montana, and Wyoming, who discusses, among other things, misconceptions of the wolf and the impact wolves have on ecology
Extended Reading: "All About Wolves"			
John Vucetich and Rolf Peterson	2012	The Wolves and Moose of Isle Royale Project	The full overview from the Isle of Royal Project from which Texts 5 and 7 are excerpted.

TEXT 1

Image Set 1

Image Set 2

Image Set 3

Image Set 4

Developing Core Literacy Proficiencies

TEXT 2

"A Brief History of Wolves in the United States"
Cornelia N. Hutt
Kids Planet

Wolves once roamed across most of North America. Over hundreds of thousands of years they **P1**
developed side by side with their **prey** and filled an important role in the web of life. **Opportunistic**
hunters, wolves preyed on deer, elk and beaver, killing and eating the young, the sick, the weak
and the old and leaving the fittest to survive and reproduce. Wolf kills provided a source of food for
5 numerous other **species** such as bears, foxes, eagles and ravens. Wolves even contributed to forest
health by keeping deer and elk populations in check, thus preventing overgrazing and soil erosion.

Not surprisingly, the cultures which inhabited North America before the time of European **P2**
exploration **revered** the wolf and its role in nature. Many **indigenous** groups relied on hunting as
their major source of food and goods and were keenly **attuned** to their environment. The elements
10 of the natural world, including the wolf, were important to their everyday lives and spirituality.

Native Americans **attributed** an **array** of powers and miracles to wolves, from the creation of **P3**
tribes to healing powers. For example, the Kwakiutl of the Pacific Northwest believed that before
they became men or women, they had been wolves. The Arikara believed that Wolf-Man made

prey	opportunistic	species
an animal hunted for food	taking advantage of a situation	a biological classification belonging to the same group
revered	**indigenous**	**attuned**
honored, adored, respected	coming from a particular region or country	aware, in harmony
attributed	**array**	
assigned, associated	a large group or number	

the Great Plains for them and the other animals. The Sioux and Cheyenne of the Great Plains and

15 many other tribes credited the wolf with teaching them how to survive by hunting and by valuing

family bonds.

In other Native American cultures, the wolf played an important role in the **spiritual** and **ceremonial**   P4

life of the tribe. Wolves were regarded as mysterious beings with powers they could **bestow** upon

people. The Crow, for instance, believed that a wolf skin could save lives. Other Native American **lore**

20 is full of stories of wolves and of wolf parts healing the sick and the **mortally** injured.

When Europeans arrived in the New World, roughly 250,000 wolves flourished in what are now the   P5

lower 48 states. Many settlers, however, brought with them a **legacy** of **persecution** dating back

centuries. Mythology, legends and fables such as those popularized by Aesop and the Brothers Grimm

intensified people's fear of wolves. In America, the killing of wolves came to symbolize the triumph

25 of civilization over what was considered to be a wilderness wasteland. In 1630, just ten years after the

Mayflower landed at Plymouth Rock, the Massachusetts Bay Colony began offering a reward (bounty)

for every wolf killed.

Colonists relied heavily on the deer population for food for themselves and as an export item. When   P6

the deer population dropped as a result of over-hunting, wolves became a convenient **scapegoat**.

30 They were also held accountable for livestock losses, even when diseases and other causes

were to blame. Few people seemed to question the belief that a safe home required the elimination

of all the wolves.

spiritual	ceremonial	bestow
beliefs and values	relating to rituals	to give as a gift
lore	**mortally**	**legacy**
traditional wise teachings or stories	ending in or causing death	something handed down from the past
persecution	**intensified**	**scapegoat**
hurting or causing trouble to someone who is weaker or different	strengthened or deepened	a person or group made to take the blame or to suffer in place of someone else

Developing Core Literacy Proficiencies

In time, wolf killing became a profession. In the 19th century, the demand for **pelts** sent hundreds P7
of hunters out to kill every wolf that they could. At the same time, ranchers moved into the western
35   plains to take advantage of cheap and abundant grazing land. As **domestic livestock** replaced the
wolf's natural prey base of bison and deer, the threat of wolf **predation** on cattle led to a massive
campaign to exterminate the wolf in the American west. Professional "wolfers" working for the
livestock industry laid out strychnine-poisoned meat lines up to 150 miles long. When populations
dropped to such low levels that wolves were difficult to find, states offered bounties with the goal
40   of **extirpating** wolves altogether. Wolves were shot, poisoned, trapped, clubbed, set on fire and
inoculated with mange, a painful and often fatal skin disease caused by mites. In a 25-year period at
the turn of the century, more than 80,000 wolves were killed in Montana alone.

Well into the 20th century, the belief that wolves posed a threat to human safety persisted despite P8
documentation to the contrary. The persecution continued. By the 1970s, only 500 to 1,000 wolves
45   remained in the lower 48 states, occupying less than three percent of their former range.

Fortunately, America's understanding of the wolf has grown in the last 20 years. As scientists have P9
discovered more about the **intricacies** of nature, our knowledge of the interdependence of all living
things has increased significantly. People are now more aware of the importance of **predators** in
maintaining healthy ecosystems. In addition, as our population has become increasingly **urbanized**
50   and wilderness areas have been swallowed up by development, we have begun to treasure what we

pelts	domestic livestock	predation
fur and skin	farm animals that are raised locally and are bred to be dependent on humans (e.g., chickens and cows)	the relationship between animals in which one hunts and feeds on the other
extirpating	**intricacies**	**predators**
removing or destroying totally	complex aspects	animals that eat other animals
urbanized		
made part of a city		

are losing. The wolf has become a symbol of our loss. The overwhelming number of wolf **advocacy** groups that now thrive in the United States attest to the degree to which these predators have captured our interest and our imagination.

Thanks to efforts by the U.S. Fish and Wildlife Service, zoos and wildlife advocacy groups, wolves P10
55 have slowly begun to recover in areas where they have long been absent. In recent years, wolves have been successfully reintroduced to former **habitats** in central Idaho, Wyoming, Montana, North Carolina and Arizona. More than 5,000 wolves now inhabit the wild south of Canada. While many welcome this recovery, a vocal minority remains strongly opposed to the presence of any wolves at all in the wild.

advocacy	habitats	
support	the natural environment; place that is natural for the life of an animal	

TEXT 3

Two Wolves
David Owens
video, search for this material online

TEXT 4

Living with Wolves
Jim and Jamie Dutcher
web page, search for this material online

Lobos of the South West
Mexican Wolves.org
web page, search for this material online

TEXT 5

"All About Wolves"
John Vucetich and Rolf Peterson
Wolves and Moose of Isle Royale Project, 2012
Excerpt

(Hunting Behavior)

Isle Royale is a remote wilderness island, isolated by the frigid waters of Lake Superior, and home to
populations of wolves and moose. As predator and prey, their lives and deaths are linked in a drama
that is timeless and historic. Their lives are historic because we have been documenting their lives for
more than five decades. This research project is the longest continuous study of any predator-prey
5 system in the world.

P1

Observations about Hunting Behavior

For most North American and European humans, eating a meal is a pretty simple affair: get some
food from the cupboard, heat it up, and eat. What if every meal required **exerting** yourself to the point
of exhaustion, holding nothing back? What if every meal meant risking serious injury or death? Under
10 these circumstances, you might be happy to eat only once a week or so—like Isle Royale wolves.

P2

Isle Royale wolves capture and kill, with their teeth, moose that are ten times their size. Think about
it for a moment—it is difficult to comprehend. A successful alpha wolf will have done this more than
one hundred times in its life.

P3

Wolves **minimize** the risk of severe injury and death by attacking the most **vulnerable** moose.
15 Somehow wolves are incredible judges of what they can handle. Wolves encounter and chase down
many moose. Chases typically continue for less than ½ a mile.

P4

exerting	minimize	vulnerable
using effort or force	to reduce in size or quantity	that can be easily hurt or attacked

Developing Core Literacy Proficiencies

During chase and **confrontation** wolves test their prey. Wolves attack only about 1 out of every   P5

ten moose that they chase down. They kill 8 or 9 of every ten moose that they decide to attack. The

decision to attack or not is a vicious tension between intense hunger and wanting not to be killed by

20 your food.

Wolves typically attack moose at the rump and nose. The strategy is to inflict injury by making   P6

large gashes in the muscle, and to slow the moose by staying attached, thereby allowing other wolves

to do the same. Eventually the moose is stopped and brought to the ground by the weight and

strength of the wolves. The cause of death may be shock or loss of blood. Feeding often begins before

25 the moose is dead.

A moose, with a wolf clamped to its rump is still **formidable**. They can easily swing around, lifting   P7

the wolf into the air, and hurl the wolf into a tree. Most experienced wolves have broken (and healed)

their ribs on several occasions. Moose deliver powerful kicks with their hooves. Wolves occasionally

die from attacking moose.

30 After a chase, wolves may kill and begin feeding within 10 or 15 minutes. Or they may wound and   P8

wait several days for the moose to die.

To some, wolves are evil for killing without cause and without eating much of what they kill. This is   P9

more a poor **rationalization** to **justify** killing wolves, than an observation rooted in fact.

Typically, wolves **consume** impressive portions of their prey, eating all but the **rumen** contents,   P10

35 larger bones, and some hair. They routinely eat what you and I would not dream of eating—the

confrontation	**formidable**	**rationalization**
encounter, argument	impressive, strong, difficult to overcome	expressed reason for doing something
justify	**consume**	**rumen**
to give a satisfactory reason or excuse for doing something	to eat or drink something entirely	the first compartment of the stomach in which food is partly digested

stomach muscles, tendons, marrow, bones, hair and hide. They typically consume 80 to 100% of all that is edible. By wolf standards, every American deer hunter is wasteful. A wolf's gut is not so different from ours that we can't appreciate what it means to resort to eating such parts.

These eating habits make sense: starvation is a very common cause of death for wolves; killing prey **P11**
40 requires a tremendous amount of energy and is a life-threatening prospect for a wolf.

Two circumstances give false impressions. First, it may take several days for a pack to consume a **P12**
carcass, or they may **cache** it and consume it later. The ultimate **utilization** of what may appear to be a poorly utilized carcass is routinely **verified** by merely revisiting the site of a moose carcass at a later date.

45 Occasionally **prey** are unusually abundant, **prone** to starvation, and easy to capture. Under such **P13**
conditions wolves may eat relatively small portions—only the most nutritious parts—of a carcass.

In this regard, wolves are no different from any other creature in the animal kingdom. Along **P14**
migration routes during spring, when song birds may be extremely abundant, hawks sometimes kill many of these birds and eat only the organs, leaving behind all the muscle. Spiders suck a smaller
50 portion of juice from their prey when prey are more common.

These are examples of an **inviolable** law of nature—utilization decreases as availability increases. **P15**
The average American[s] throw[] away about 15% of all the **edible** food that they purchase. Ten percent of our landfills are food that was once edible.

carcass	cache	utilization
dead body of an animal	conceal; hide	use
verified	**prey**	**prone**
proven to be true	an animal that is hunted for food by another animal	doing something often, having a habit
inviolable	**edible**	
unbreakable	that can be eaten as food	

Finally, waste is a matter of perspective. What wolves leave behind, **scavengers invariably** utilize. **P16**

55 Foxes, eagles, and ravens are among the most important scavengers on Isle Royale. However, even
smaller scavengers may benefit greatly. To a chickadee, for example, a moose carcass is the world's
largest **suet ball**. Scavengers make waste an impossibility.

After feeding for a few hours on a fresh kill, wolves sprawl out or curl up in the snow and sleep. To **P17**
eat a large meal with one's family, and then to rest. To stretch out and just rest. When we observe

60 wolves during the winter, about 30% of the time they are just sleeping or resting near a recent kill.
Wolves have plenty of reason to rest.

When wolves are active, they are really active. On a daily basis, wolves burn about 70% more **P18**
calories compared to typical animals of similar size.

While chasing and attacking a moose, a wolf may burn calories at ten to twenty times the rate they **P19**

65 do while resting. Its heart beats at five times its resting rate. For context, a world class athlete can
burn calories at no more than about five times the calories they burn at rest. The intensity at which
wolves work while hunting is far beyond the **capabilities** of a human.

While spending all this energy, wolves may eat only once every five to ten days. During the time **P20**
between kills a wolf may lose as much as 8–10% of its body weight. However, a wolf can regain all of

70 this lost weight in just two days of **ad libitum** eating and resting.

When food is plentiful, wolves spend a substantial amount of time simply resting, because they can. **P21**
When food is scarce, wolves spend much time resting because they need to.

scavengers	invariably	suet ball
animals that feed on dead animals	unchanging; constantly	a ball of food prepared for birds
capabilities	**ad libitum**	
abilities	a time of pleasure	

Wolves work tremendously hard, but they also take resting very seriously.   **P22**

In some important ways, wolves and humans are alike. We are both social, intelligent, and   **P23**
75 communicative. In other ways, we differ. With thoughtful **reflection**, however, we can understand
or imagine some of these aspects of a wolf's life—their endless walking and their feast or famine
lifestyle.

However, in a fundamental way wolves **perceive** a world that is simply beyond our comprehension   **P24**
and imagination. Through their noses, wolves sense and know things that we could never know.

80 We can build tools to help us visualize things we can't see directly, like x-ray telescopes and electron   **P25**
microscopes. However, it is difficult to imagine a tool that would allow us to sense or experience the
olfactory world experienced by the everyday life of a wolf.

Wolves have 280 million olfactory receptors in their nasal passages—more than the number of   **P26**
visual receptors in their **retinas**. Wolves can detect odors that are hundreds to millions of times
85 fainter than what humans can detect.

A wolf often walks with its head down, nose close to the ground. Wolves rely on their noses for two   **P27**
of the most basic activities—hunting and communicating with other wolves. Smells, more than sights
or sounds, determine where a wolf will travel next.

reflection	perceive	olfactory
attention, scrutiny	observe, realize, understand	relating to the sense of smell
retinas		
the most inner part of the eyeballs that receive the images through the lens		

While hunting, moose are most often detected first by smell. Wolves commonly hunt into the wind, and by doing so can smell moose from 300 yards away.

90

P28

A moose with jaw **necrosis** is vulnerable, and wolves can almost certainly smell that a moose has jaw necrosis before even seeing it.

P29

The life of a wolf is difficult and typically, short. The chances of pup survival are highly variable. In some years, for some packs, most or all pups die. In other years, most or all survive.

P30

95

Of the wolves that survive their first six to nine months, most are dead by three or four years of age. Every year, one in four or five adult wolves dies in a healthy wolf population.

P31

Alpha wolves tend to be the longest lived. They commonly live for between six and nine years. Of the pups that survive their first year, only about one or two of every ten rise to the level of alpha. Most die without ever reproducing, and few wolves ever live long enough to grow old.

P32

100

These rates of **mortality** are normal, even when humans are not involved in the death of wolves.

P33

Wolves are **intensely social**. They are born into a family, and spend most of their time with other wolves. Wolves know each other, and they know each other well. Imagine a world where it is common for one out of every four or five of the people you know to die.

P34

necrosis	mortality	intensely
rot or gangrene; dead tissue	death	greatly
social		
seeking or enjoying the companionship of others		

The causes of wolf death are primarily lack of food and being killed by other wolves in conflict over P35
105 food. This fact denies all **credibility** to **perceiving** wolves as wasteful **gluttons**, as they are often
portrayed.

Most wolves die in the process of **dispersing**. Dispersal is a tremendous risk, but one worth taking. P36
Ultimately, the only thing that matters is reproducing. Reproduction is very unlikely within the pack
to which a wolf is born. It is better to risk death for some chance of finding a mate and a territory than
110 to live safely but have virtually no chance of reproduction.

credibility	perceiving	gluttons
having the ability to be believed or trusted	observing, understanding	people who eat and drink more than they need, in excess
dispersing		
the act of separating or moving away		

TEXT 6

White Fang
Jack London
Macmillan, 1906

Excerpt: Pt. II, Ch. I, "The Battle of the Fangs"

It was the she-wolf who had first caught the sound of men's voices and the whining of the sled-dogs; **P1**
and it was the she-wolf who was first to spring away from the cornered man in his circle of dying
flame. The pack had been **loath** to **forego** the kill it had hunted down, and it lingered for several
minutes, making sure of the sounds, and then it, too, sprang away on the trail made by the she-wolf.

5 Running at the forefront of the pack was a large grey wolf—one of its several leaders. It was he who **P2**
directed the pack's course on the heels of the she-wolf. It was he who snarled warningly at the younger
members of the pack or slashed at them with his fangs when they **ambitiously** tried to pass him. And it
was he who increased the pace when he sighted the she-wolf, now trotting slowly across the snow.

She dropped in alongside by him, as though it were her **appointed** position, and took the pace of **P3**
10 the pack. He did not snarl at her, nor show his teeth, when any leap of hers chanced to put her in
advance of him. On the contrary, he seemed kindly **disposed** toward her—too kindly to suit her, for
he was prone to run near to her, and when he ran too near it was she who snarled and showed her
teeth. Nor was she above slashing his shoulder sharply on occasion. At such times he betrayed no
anger. He merely sprang to the side and ran stiffly ahead for several awkward leaps, in carriage and
15 conduct resembling an **abashed** country **swain**.

loath	forego	ambitiously
reluctant	to leave without finishing	eagerly, with effort
appointed	**disposed**	**abashed**
nominated, selected, given	willing, showing good temper	humble, lower in rank
swain		
a male admirer or lover		

This was his one trouble in the running of the pack; but she had other troubles. On her other side   P4
ran a **gaunt** old wolf, grizzled and marked with the scars of many battles. He ran always on her right
side. The fact that he had but one eye, and that the left eye, might account for this. He, also, was
addicted to crowding her, to **veering** toward her till his scarred muzzle touched her body, or shoulder,
20   or neck. As with the running mate on the left, she **repelled** these attentions with her teeth; but when
both bestowed their attentions at the same time she was roughly **jostled**, being compelled, with
quick snaps to either side, to drive both lovers away and at the same time to maintain her forward
leap with the pack and see the way of her feet before her. At such times her running mates flashed
their teeth and growled threateningly across at each other. They might have fought, but even **wooing**
25   and its rivalry waited upon the more pressing hunger-need of the pack.

After each **repulse**, when the old wolf sheered abruptly away from the sharp-toothed object of his   P5
desire, he shouldered against a young three-year-old that ran on his blind right side. This young
wolf had attained his full size; and, considering the weak and **famished** condition of the pack, he
possessed more than the average **vigour** and spirit. Nevertheless, he ran with his head even with
30   the shoulder of his one-eyed elder. When he ventured to run abreast of the older wolf (which was
seldom), a snarl and a snap sent him back even with the shoulder again. Sometimes, however, he
dropped cautiously and slowly behind and edged in between the old leader and the she-wolf. This
was doubly resented, even triply resented. When she snarled her displeasure, the old leader would
whirl on the three-year-old. Sometimes she whirled with him. And sometimes the young leader on the
35   left whirled, too.

gaunt	veering	repelled
underweight and bony from lack of food	changing direction or course	driven or forced backwards
jostled	**wooing**	**repulse**
shoved roughly	trying to win or see the affection or love of someone	repel, force away
famished	**vigour**	
extremely hungry	energy	

At such times, confronted by three sets of savage teeth, the young wolf stopped **precipitately**, P6
throwing himself back on his **haunches**, with fore-legs stiff, mouth menacing, and mane bristling.
This confusion in the front of the moving pack always caused confusion in the rear. The wolves behind
collided with the young wolf and expressed their displeasure by administering sharp nips on his
40 hind-legs and **flanks**. He was laying up trouble for himself, for lack of food and short tempers went
together; but with the boundless faith of youth he persisted in repeating the maneuver every little
while, though it never succeeded in gaining anything for him but **discomfiture**.

Had there been food, mating and fighting would have gone on apace, and the pack-formation P7
would have been broken up. But the situation of the pack was desperate. It was lean with long-
45 standing hunger. It ran below its ordinary speed. At the rear limped the weak members, the very
young and the very old. At the front were the strongest. Yet all were more like skeletons than full-
bodied wolves. Nevertheless, with the exception of the ones that limped, the movements of the
animals were effortless and tireless. Their stringy muscles seemed founts of **inexhaustible** energy.
Behind every steel-like contraction of a muscle, lay another steel-like contraction, and another, and
50 another, apparently without end.

They ran many miles that day. They ran through the night. And the next day found them still P8
running. They were running over the surface of a world frozen and dead. No life stirred. They alone
moved through the vast **inertness**. They alone were alive, and they sought for other things that were
alive in order that they might **devour** them and continue to live.

55 They crossed low divides and ranged a dozen small streams in a lower-lying country before their P9
quest was rewarded. Then they came upon moose. It was a big bull they first found. Here was meat and

precipitately	haunches	flanks
quickly	hindquarters of an animal	the sides of an animal
discomfiture	**inexhaustible**	**inertness**
frustration of hopes or plans	can not be tired	lifelessness
devour		
to swallow or eat with hunger		

life, and it was guarded by no mysterious fires nor flying missiles of flame. Splay hoofs and **palmated**

antlers they knew, and they flung their customary patience and caution to the wind. It was a brief fight

and fierce. The big bull was beset on every side. He ripped them open or split their skulls with shrewdly

60 driven blows of his great hoofs. He crushed them and broke them on his large horns. He stamped them

into the snow under him in the wallowing struggle. But he was **foredoomed**, and he went down with

the she-wolf tearing savagely at his throat, and with other teeth fixed everywhere upon him, devouring

him alive, before ever his last struggles ceased or his last damage had been wrought.

There was food in plenty. The bull weighed over eight hundred pounds—fully twenty pounds of   **P10**

65 meat per mouth for the forty-odd wolves of the pack. But if they could fast prodigiously, they could

feed **prodigiously**, and soon a few scattered bones were all that remained of the splendid live brute

that had faced the pack a few hours before.

There was now much resting and sleeping. With full stomachs, bickering and quarrelling began   **P11**

among the younger males, and this continued through the few days that followed before the

70 breaking-up of the pack. The **famine** was over. The wolves were now in the country of game, and

though they still hunted in pack, they hunted more cautiously, cutting out heavy cows or crippled old

bulls from the small moose-herds they ran across.

There came a day, in this land of plenty, when the wolf-pack split in half and went in different   **P12**

directions. The she-wolf, the young leader on her left, and the one-eyed elder on her right, led their

75 half of the pack down to the Mackenzie River and across into the lake country to the east. Each

day this **remnant** of the pack **dwindled**. Two by two, male and female, the wolves were deserting.

Occasionally a solitary male was driven out by the sharp teeth of his rivals. In the end there remained

only four: the she-wolf, the young leader, the one-eyed one, and the ambitious three-year-old.

palmated	foredoomed	prodigiously
shaped like an open palm	doomed or condemned beforehand	enormously
famine	**remnant**	**dwindled**
extreme hunger or starvation	small part of something leftover	became less or fewer

The she-wolf had by now developed a ferocious temper. Her three suitors all bore the marks of her **P13**

80 teeth. Yet they never replied in kind, never defended themselves against her. They turned their

shoulders to her most savage slashes, and with wagging tails and **mincing** steps strove to **placate**

her wrath. But if they were all mildness toward her, they were all fierceness toward one another. The

three-year-old grew too ambitious in his fierceness. He caught the one-eyed elder on his blind side

and ripped his ear into ribbons. Though the grizzled old fellow could see only on one side, against

85 the youth and vigor of the other he brought into play the wisdom of long years of experience. His lost

eye and his scarred muzzle bore evidence to the nature of his experience. He had survived too many

battles to be in doubt for a moment about what to do.

The battle began fairly, but it did not end fairly. There was no telling what the outcome would have **P14**

been, for the third wolf joined the elder, and together, old leader and young leader, they attacked the

90 ambitious three-year-old and proceeded to destroy him. He was **beset** on either side by the merciless

fangs of his **erstwhile** comrades. Forgotten were the days they had hunted together, the game they

had pulled down, the famine they had suffered. That business was a thing of the past. The business of

love was at hand—ever a sterner and crueler business than that of food-getting.

And in the meanwhile, the she-wolf, the cause of it all, sat down contentedly on her haunches and **P15**

95 watched. She was even pleased. This was her day—and it came not often—when manes bristled, and

fang smote fang or ripped and tore the yielding flesh, all for the possession of her.

And in the business of love the three-year-old, who had made this his first adventure upon it, yielded **P16**

up his life. On either side of his body stood his two rivals. They were gazing at the she-wolf, who sat

smiling in the snow. But the elder leader was wise, very wise, in love even as in battle. The younger

100 leader turned his head to lick a wound on his shoulder. The curve of his neck was turned toward his

rival. With his one eye the elder saw the opportunity. He darted in low and closed with his fangs. It

mincing	placate	beset
acting dainty, nice, or elegant	calm or quiet	to hem in or surround
erstwhile		
previous		

was a long, ripping slash, and deep as well. His teeth, in passing, burst the wall of the great vein of the throat. Then he leaped clear.

The young leader snarled terribly, but his snarl broke midmost into a tickling cough. Bleeding and   **P17**
105 coughing, already stricken, he sprang at the elder and fought while life faded from him, his legs going weak beneath him, the light of day dulling on his eyes, his blows and springs falling shorter and shorter.

And all the while the she-wolf sat on her haunches and smiled. She was made glad in **vague** ways by   **P18**
the battle, for this was the mating of the Wild, the tragedy of the natural world that was tragedy only to those that died. To those that survived it was not tragedy, but realization and achievement.

110 When the young leader lay in the snow and moved no more, One Eye stalked over to the she-wolf.   **P19**
His **carriage** was one of mingled triumph and caution. He was plainly expectant of a **rebuff**, and he was just as plainly surprised when her teeth did not flash out at him in anger. For the first time she met him with a kindly manner. She sniffed noses with him, and even **condescended** to leap about and frisk and play with him in quite puppyish fashion. And he, for all his grey years and **sage** experience,
115 behaved quite as puppyishly and even a little more foolishly.

Forgotten already were the **vanquished** rivals and the love-tale red-written on the snow. Forgotten,   **P20**
save once, when old One Eye stopped for a moment to lick his stiffening wounds. Then it was that his lips half **writhed** into a snarl, and the hair of his neck and shoulders involuntarily bristled, while he half crouched for a spring, his claws **spasmodically** clutching into the snow-surface for firmer footing. But
120 it was all forgotten the next moment, as he sprang after the she-wolf, who was **coyly** leading him a chase through the woods.

vague	carriage	rebuff
not clear or definite	appearance, look	snub or rejection
condescended	**sage**	**vanquished**
did something that she thought was below her dignity	wise	beaten, overcome
writhed	**spasmodically**	**coyly**
twisted or bent out of shape	with bursts of excitement	timidly

  Developing Core Literacy Proficiencies

TEXT 7

"All About Wolves"
John Vucetich and Rolf Peterson
Wolves and Moose of Isle Royale Project, 2012
Excerpt

(Pack Behavior)

Isle Royale is a remote wilderness island, **isolated** by the frigid waters of Lake Superior, and home to   **P1**
populations of wolves and moose. As predator and prey, their lives and deaths are linked in a drama
that is timeless and historic. Their lives are historic because we have been documenting their lives for
more than five decades. This research project is the longest continuous study of any predator-prey
5 system in the world.

Observations of Pack Behavior

Wolves develop from pups at an incredible rate. Pups are born, in late April, after just a two-month   **P2**
pregnancy. They are born deaf, blind, and weigh no more than a can of soda pop. At this time, pups
can do basically just one thing—**suckle** their mother's milk.

10 Within a month, pups can hear and see, weigh ten pounds, and explore and play around the den site.   **P3**
The parents and sometimes one- or two-year-old **siblings** bring food back to the den site. The food is
regurgitated for the pups to eat. By about two months of age (late June), pups are fully weaned and
eat only meat. By three months of age (late July), pups travel as much as a few miles to **rendezvous**
sites, where pups wait for adults to return from hunts.

isolated	suckle	siblings
separated from other persons or things	to suck at the breast or udder	brothers or sisters
regurgitated	**rendezvous**	
undigested food that is vomited	a place that is popular to meet or gather	

15 Pups surviving to six or seven months of age (late September) have adult teeth, are eighty percent   **P4**

their full size, and travel with the pack for many miles as they hunt and patrol their territory. When

food is plentiful, most pups survive to their first birthday. As often, food is scarce and no pups survive.

A wolf may disperse from its **natal** pack when it is as young as 12 months old. In some cases a wolf   **P5**

might disperse and breed when it is 22 months old—the second February of its life. In any event, from

20 12 months of age onward, wolves look for a chance to **disperse** and mate with a wolf from another

pack. In the meantime, they bide their time in the safety of their natal pack.

From birth until his or her last dying day, a wolf is **inextricably** linked to other wolves in a **complex**   **P6**

web of social relationships. The ultimate basis for these relationships is sharing food with some,

depriving it from others, reproducing with another, and suppressing reproduction among others.

25 Most wolves live in packs, a community sharing daily life with three to eleven other wolves. Core   **P7**

pack members are an **alpha** pair and their pups. Other members commonly include **offspring** from

previous years, and occasionally other less closely related wolves.

Pups depend on food from their parents. Relationships among older, physically mature offspring   **P8**

are fundamentally tense. These wolves want to **mate**, but alphas **repress** any attempts to mate. So,

30 mating typically requires leaving the pack. However, **dispersal** is dangerous. While biding time for a

natal	disperse	inextricably
relating to birth	to separate, to move away	completely involved in something
complex	**alpha**	**offspring**
a very complicated arrangement	an animal having the highest rank in its group	children or young of a certain parent
mate	**repress**	**dispersal**
to reproduce	to keep down, to stop	the act of dispersing, separating, moving away

good opportunity to disperse, these **subordinate** wolves want the safety and food that come from pack living. They are sometimes tolerated by the alpha wolves, to varying degrees. The degree of **tolerance** depends on the degree of obedience and submission to the will of alpha wolves. For a subordinate wolf, the choice, typically, is to **acquiesce** or leave the pack.

35 Alphas lead travels and hunts. They feed first, and they **exclude** from feeding whomever they choose. P9
Maintaining alpha **status** requires controlling the behavior of pack mates. Occasionally a subordinate wolf is strong enough to take over the alpha position.

Wolf families have and know about their neighbors. Alphas exclude non-pack members from their P10
territory, and try to kill trespassers. Mature, subordinate pack members are sometimes less hostile to
40 outside wolves—they are **potential** mates.

Being an alpha wolf requires aggression, control, and leadership. Perhaps not surprisingly, alpha P11
wolves typically possess higher levels of stress hormones than do subordinate wolves, who may not eat as much, but have, apparently, far less stress.

Pack members are usually, but not always friendly and cooperative. Wolves from other packs are P12
45 usually, but not always enemies. Managing all of these relationships, in a way that minimizes the risk of injury and death to one's self, requires **sophisticated** communication. Accurately interpreting and judging these communications requires intelligence. Communication and intelligence

subordinate	tolerance	acquiesce
belonging to a lower rank	acceptance, patient attitude	to accept something without any protest
exclude	**status**	**potential**
to keep out	the position of an individual in relation to others in the group	possible
sophisticated		
complex or complicated		

are needed to know who my friends and enemies are, where they are, and what may be their **intentions**. These may be the reasons that most social animals, including humans, are intelligent and
50 communicative.

Like humans, wolves communicate with voices. Pack mates often separate temporarily. When they   **P13**
want to rejoin they often howl. They say: "Hey, where are you guys? I'm over here." Wolf packs also
howl to tell other packs: "Hey, we are over here; stay away from us, or else."

There is so much more to wolf communication. Scientists recognize at least ten different   **P14**
55 categories of sound (e.g., howls, growls, barks, etc.). Each is believed to communicate a different,
context-dependent message. Wolves also have an elaborate body language. As **subtle** as body
language can be, even scientists recognize communication to be taking place by the positions
of about fifteen different body parts (e.g., ears, tail, teeth, etc.). Each body part can hold one
of several positions (e.g., tail up, out, down, etc.). There could easily be hundreds to thousands
60 of different messages communicated by different combinations of these body positions and
vocal noises. Scientists **apprehend** (or misapprehend) just a fraction of what wolves are able
to communicate to each other.

Wolves also communicate with scent. The most distinctive use of scent entails territorial   **P15**
scent marking.

65 **Elusiveness** makes wolves mysterious. This is true and fine. However, true love cannot survive   **P16**
mystery due to ignorance. Mature love requires knowledge. In some basic ways the life of a wolf is
very ordinary, even **mundane**, and its comprehension is fully within our grasp if we just focus.

intentions	subtle	apprehend
purposes or goals	not obvious, can be difficult to understand or see	to understand the meaning of something
elusiveness	**mundane**	
the quality of being difficult to see	dull	

The life of a wolf is largely occupied with walking. Wolves are tremendous walkers. Day after day, **P17** wolves commonly walk for eight hours a day, averaging five miles per hour. They commonly travel
70 thirty miles a day, and may walk 4,000 miles a year.

Wolves living in packs walk for two basic reasons—to capture food and to defend their territories. **P18** Isle Royale wolf territories average about 75 square miles. This is small compared to some wolf populations, where territories can be as large as 500 square miles. To patrol and defend even a small territory involves a never-ending amount of walking. Week after week, wolves cover the same trails. It
75 must seem very ordinary.

The average North American human walks two to three miles per day. A fit human walks at least five **P19** miles/day. If you want to know more about the life of a wolf, spend more time just walking, and while walking, know that you are walking. What do wolves think about much while walking?

Wolves defend territories. About once a week, wolves patrol most of their territorial boundary. About **P20**
80 every two to three hundred yards along the territorial boundary an alpha wolf will scent mark, that is, urinate or defecate in a conspicuous location. The odor from this mark is detectable, even to a human nose, a week or two after being deposited. The mark communicates to potential trespassing wolves that this area is defended. Territorial defense is a matter of life and death. Intruding wolves, if detected, are chased off or killed, if possible.

85 Wolves are like humans for having such complex family relationships. Wolves are also like some **P21** humans in that they wage complete warfare toward their neighbors. An alpha wolf typically kills one to three wolves in his or her lifetime.

TEXT 8

White Fang
Jack London
Macmillan, 1906

Excerpt: Pt II., Ch. III, "The Grey Cub"

He was different from his brothers and sisters. Their hair already **betrayed** the reddish hue inherited   **P1**
from their mother, the she-wolf; while he alone, in this particular, took after his father. He was the
one little grey cub of the litter. He had bred true to the straight wolf-stock—in fact, he had bred true
to old One Eye himself, physically, with but a single exception, and that was he had two eyes to his
5 father's one.

The grey cub's eyes had not been open long, yet already he could see with steady clearness. And   **P2**
while his eyes were still closed, he had felt, tasted, and smelled. He knew his two brothers and his
two sisters very well. He had begun to **romp** with them in a **feeble**, awkward way, and even to
squabble, his little throat vibrating with a queer **rasping** noise (the **forerunner** of the growl), as he
10 worked himself into a **passion**. And long before his eyes had opened he had learned by touch, taste,
and smell to know his mother—a fount of warmth and liquid food and tenderness. She possessed a
gentle, caressing tongue that soothed him when it passed over his soft little body, and that impelled
him to snuggle close against her and to doze off to sleep.

Most of the first month of his life had been passed thus in sleeping; but now he could see quite well,   **P3**
15 and he stayed awake for longer periods of time, and he was coming to learn his world quite well. His

betrayed	romp	feeble
revealed, exposed, gave away	to run without force or effort	physically weak, without strength
rasping	**forerunner**	**passion**
a harsh grating sound	coming before	strong emotion

world was gloomy; but he did not know that, for he knew no other world. It was dim-lighted; but his eyes had never had to adjust themselves to any other light. His world was very small. Its limits were the walls of the **lair**; but as he had no knowledge of the wide world outside, he was never **oppressed** by the narrow **confines** of his existence.

20 But he had early discovered that one wall of his world was different from the rest. This was the mouth **P4** of the cave and the source of light. He had discovered that it was different from the other walls long before he had any thoughts of his own, any **conscious volitions.** It had been an irresistible attraction before ever his eyes opened and looked upon it. The light from it had beat upon his sealed lids, and the eyes and the optic nerves had pulsated to little, sparklike flashes, warm-coloured and strangely
25 pleasing. The life of his body, and of every fibre of his body, the life that was the very substance of his body and that was apart from his own personal life, had **yearned** toward this light and urged his body toward it in the same way that the **cunning** chemistry of a plant urges it toward the sun.

Always, in the beginning, before his conscious life dawned, he had crawled toward the mouth of **P5** the cave. And in this his brothers and sisters were one with him. Never, in that period, did any of
30 them crawl toward the dark corners of the back-wall. The light drew them as if they were plants; the chemistry of the life that composed them demanded the light as a necessity of being; and their little puppet-bodies crawled blindly and chemically, like the tendrils of a vine. Later on, when each developed individuality and became personally conscious of **impulsions** and desires, the attraction of the light increased. They were always crawling and sprawling toward it, and being driven back
35 from it by their mother.

lair	oppressed	confines
den or sleeping area of a wild animal	tormented, frustrated	limits and boarders
conscious	**volitions**	**yearned**
aware	choices or decisions made by the will	desired, wanted
cunning	**impulsions**	
skillful, crafty	inner compulsions, urges	

It was in this way that the grey cub learned other **attributes** of his mother than the soft, soothing,   P6

tongue. In his insistent crawling toward the light, he discovered in her a nose that with a sharp nudge

administered **rebuke**, and later, a paw, that crushed him down and rolled him over and over with

swift, **calculating** stroke. Thus he learned hurt; and on top of it he learned to avoid hurt, first, by not

40 **incurring** the risk of it; and second, when he had incurred the risk, by dodging and by retreating.

These were conscious actions, and were the results of his first generalisations upon the world. Before

that he had **recoiled** automatically from hurt, as he had crawled automatically toward the light. After

that he recoiled from hurt because he knew that it was hurt.

He was a fierce little cub. So were his brothers and sisters. It was to be expected. He was a carnivorous   P7

45 animal. He came of a breed of meat-killers and meat-eaters. His father and mother lived wholly upon

meat. The milk he had sucked with his first flickering life, was milk transformed directly from meat,

and now, at a month old, when his eyes had been open for but a week, he was beginning himself to

eat meat—meat half-digested by the she-wolf and **disgorged** for the five growing cubs that already

made too great demand upon her breast.

50 But he was, further, the fiercest of the **litter**. He could make a louder rasping growl than any of them.   P8

His tiny **rages** were much more terrible than theirs. It was he that first learned the trick of rolling a

fellow-cub over with a **cunning** paw-stroke. And it was he that first gripped another cub by the ear

and pulled and tugged and growled through jaws tight-clenched. And certainly it was he that caused

the mother the most trouble in keeping her litter from the mouth of the cave.

attributes	rebuke	calculating
qualities or characteristics	stern disapproval	selfishly scheming or planning
incurring	**recoiled**	**disgorged**
provoking	drawn back; started back as caused by alarm or disgust	vomited
litter	**rages**	**cunning**
the name given to multiple young of an animal born at the same time	fits of violent anger	skillful

55 The fascination of the light for the grey cub increased from day to day. He was perpetually departing   P9

on yard-long adventures toward the cave's entrance, and as perpetually being driven back. Only he did

not know it for an entrance. He did not know anything about entrances—passages whereby one goes

from one place to another place. He did not know any other place, much less of a way to get there. So

to him the entrance of the cave was a wall—a wall of light. As the sun was to the outside dweller, this

60 wall was to him the sun of his world. It attracted him as a candle attracts a moth. He was always striving

to attain it. The life that was so swiftly expanding within him, urged him continually toward the wall of

light. The life that was within him knew that it was the one way out, the way he was **predestined** to

tread. But he himself did not know anything about it. He did not know there was any outside at all.

There was one strange thing about this wall of light. His father (he had already come to recognise his   P10

65 father as the one other dweller in the world, a creature like his mother, who slept near the light and

was a bringer of meat)—his father had a way of walking right into the white far wall and disappearing.

The grey cub could not understand this. Though never permitted by his mother to approach that wall,

he had approached the other walls, and encountered hard obstruction on the end of his tender nose.

This hurt. And after several such adventures, he left the walls alone. Without thinking about it, he

70 accepted this disappearing into the wall as a **peculiarity** of his father, as milk and half-digested meat

were peculiarities of his mother.

In fact, the grey cub was not given to thinking—at least, to the kind of thinking customary of men.   P11

His brain worked in dim ways. Yet his conclusions were as sharp and distinct as those achieved

by men. He had a method of accepting things, without questioning the why and wherefore. In

75 reality, this was the act of classification. He was never disturbed over why a thing happened. How it

happened was sufficient for him. Thus, when he had bumped his nose on the back-wall a few times,

he accepted that he would not disappear into walls. In the same way he accepted that his father could

predestined	tread	peculiarity
determined beforehand	to walk or stride—to put the foot down	a habit or characteristic

disappear into walls. But he was not in the least disturbed by desire to find out the reason for the difference between his father and himself. **Logic** and **physics** were no part of his mental make-up.

80 Like most creatures of the Wild, he early experienced famine. There came a time when not only did   P12
the meat-supply cease, but the milk no longer came from his mother's breast. At first, the cubs whimpered and cried, but for the most part they slept. It was not long before they were reduced to a coma of hunger. There were no more spats and squabbles, no more tiny rages nor attempts at growling; while the adventures toward the far white wall **ceased** altogether. The cubs slept, while the

85 life that was in them flickered and died down.

One Eye was desperate. He ranged far and wide, and slept but little in the lair that had now become   P13
cheerless and miserable. The she-wolf, too, left her litter and went out in search of meat. In the first days after the birth of the cubs, One Eye had journeyed several times back to the Indian camp and robbed the rabbit snares; but, with the melting of the snow and the opening of the streams, the

90 Indian camp had moved away, and that source of supply was closed to him.

When the grey cub came back to life and again took interest in the far white wall, he found that the   P14
population of his world had been reduced. Only one sister remained to him. The rest were gone. As he grew stronger, he found himself **compelled** to play alone, for the sister no longer lifted her head nor moved about. His little body rounded out with the meat he now ate; but the food had come too late

95 for her. She slept continuously, a tiny skeleton flung round with skin in which the flame flickered lower and lower and at last went out.

logic	physics	ceased
a valid way of reasoning	science that studies matter and energy and seeks answers by experimenting and observing	stopped, finished
compelled		
forced to do something		

Then there came a time when the grey cub no longer saw his father appearing and disappearing in   P15
the wall nor lying down asleep in the entrance. This had happened at the end of a second and less
severe famine. The she-wolf knew why One Eye never came back, but there was no way by which she
100 could tell what she had seen to the grey cub. Hunting herself for meat, up the left fork of the stream
where lived the lynx, she had followed a day-old trail of One Eye. And she had found him, or what
remained of him, at the end of the trail. There were many signs of the battle that had been fought,
and of the lynx's withdrawal to her lair after having won the victory. Before she went away, the
she-wolf had found this lair, but the signs told her that the lynx was inside, and she had not dared
105 to venture in.

After that, the she-wolf in her hunting avoided the left fork. For she knew that in the lynx's lair was a   P16
litter of kittens, and she knew the lynx for a fierce, bad-tempered creature and a terrible fighter. It was
all very well for half a dozen wolves to drive a lynx, spitting and bristling, up a tree; but it was quite a
different matter for a lone wolf to encounter a lynx—especially when the lynx was known to have a
110 litter of hungry kittens at her back.

But the Wild is the Wild, and motherhood is motherhood, at all times fiercely protective whether in   P17
the Wild or out of it; and the time was to come when the she-wolf, for her grey cub's sake, would
venture the left fork, and the lair in the rocks, and the lynx's **wrath**.

wrath		
fierce anger		

TEXT 9

"We Didn't Domesticate Dogs.
They Domesticated Us."
Brian Hare and Vanessa Woods
National Geographic News, 2013

In the story of how the dog came in from the cold and onto our sofas, we tend to give ourselves a **P1** little too much credit. The most common **assumption** is that some **hunter-gatherer** with a soft spot for cuteness found some wolf puppies and adopted them. Over time, these tamed wolves would have shown their **prowess** at hunting, so humans kept them around the campfire until they **evolved** into

5 dogs. (See "How to Build a Dog.")

But when we look back at our relationship with wolves throughout history, this doesn't really make **P2** sense. For one thing, the wolf was **domesticated** at a time when modern humans were not very **tolerant** of **carnivorous** competitors. In fact, after modern humans arrived in Europe around 43,000 years ago, they pretty much wiped out every large carnivore that existed, including saber-toothed

10 cats and giant hyenas.

assumption	hunter-gatherer	prowess
something that is believed to be true	someone who hunts animals and forages food from the land rather than through agriculture	great ability or skill
evolved	**domesticated**	**tolerant**
to change slowly into a better, more complex, or more advanced state	what was once wild is now tame	to accept something unpleasant or displeasing
carnivorous		
a meat eater		

The fossil record doesn't reveal whether these large carnivores starved to death because modern humans took most of the meat or whether humans picked them off on purpose. Either way, most of the **Ice Age bestiary** went extinct.

The hunting hypothesis, that humans used wolves to hunt, doesn't hold up either. Humans were **P3** already successful hunters without wolves, more successful than every other large carnivore. Wolves eat a lot of meat, as much as one deer per ten wolves every day—a lot for humans to feed or compete against. And anyone who has seen wolves in a feeding frenzy knows that wolves don't like to share.

Humans have a long history of **eradicating** wolves, rather than trying to adopt them. Over the last **P4** few centuries, almost every culture has hunted wolves to extinction. The first written record of the wolf's **persecution** was in the sixth century b.c. when Solon of Athens offered a bounty for every wolf killed. The last wolf was killed in England in the 16th century under the order of Henry VII. In Scotland, the **forested** landscape made wolves more difficult to kill. In response, the Scots burned the forests. North American wolves were not much better off. By 1930, there was not a wolf left in the 48 **contiguous** states of America. (See "Wolf Wars.")

If this is a snapshot of our behavior toward wolves over the centuries, it presents one of the most **P5** **perplexing** problems: How was this misunderstood creature tolerated by humans long enough to evolve into the domestic dog?

Ice Age	bestiary	eradicating
an era when the Earth was mostly covered by ice	referring to a group of beasts or animal species	to completely remove something
persecution	**forested**	**contiguous**
to treat a certain group or individual unfairly	filled with trees	directly next to or touching
perplexing		
confusing, hard to understand		

The short version is that we often think of evolution as being the survival of the fittest, where the **P6** strong and the dominant survive and the soft and weak **perish.** But essentially, far from the survival of

30 the leanest and meanest, the success of dogs comes down to survival of the friendliest.

Most likely, it was wolves that approached us, not the other way around, probably while they were **P7** scavenging around garbage dumps on the edge of human settlements. The wolves that were bold but aggressive would have been killed by humans, and so only the ones that were bold and friendly would have been tolerated.

35 Friendliness caused strange things to happen in the wolves. They started to look different. **P8** Domestication gave them splotchy coats, floppy ears, wagging tails. In only several generations, these friendly wolves would have become very distinctive from their more aggressive relatives. But the changes did not just affect their looks. Changes also happened to their psychology. These **protodogs** evolved the ability to read human gestures.

40 As dog owners, we take for granted that we can point to a ball or toy and our dog will bound off to **P9** get it. But the ability of dogs to read human **gestures** is remarkable.

Even our closest relatives—chimpanzees and **bonobos**—can't read our gestures as readily as dogs **P10** can. Dogs are remarkably similar to human infants in the way they pay attention to us. This ability accounts for the extraordinary communication we have with our dogs. Some dogs are so attuned to

45 their owners that they can read a gesture as subtle as a change in eye direction.

perish	protodogs	gestures
to die	The first wolf dogs to become human companions	moving parts of the body to convey meaning
bonobos		
a species of great ape		

Developing Core Literacy Proficiencies

With this new ability, these protodogs were worth knowing. People who had dogs during a hunt would likely have had an advantage over those who didn't. Even today, tribes in Nicaragua depend on dogs to detect prey. Moose hunters in alpine regions bring home 56 percent more prey when they are accompanied by dogs. In the Congo, hunters believe they would starve without their dogs. **P11**

50 Dogs would also have served as a warning system, barking at **hostile** strangers from neighboring tribes. They could have defended their humans from predators. **P12**

And finally, though this is not a pleasant thought, when times were tough, dogs could have served as an emergency food supply. Thousands of years before refrigeration and with no crops to store, hunter-gatherers had no food reserves until the domestication of dogs. In tough times, dogs that **P13**

55 were the least efficient hunters might have been sacrificed to save the group or the best hunting dogs. Once humans realized the usefulness of keeping dogs as an emergency food supply, it was not a huge jump to realize plants could be used in a similar way.

So, far from a **benign** human adopting a wolf puppy, it is more likely that a population of wolves adopted us. As the advantages of dog ownership became clear, we were as strongly affected by our **P14**

60 relationship with them as they have been by their relationship with us. Dogs may even have been the **catalyst** for our civilization.

hostile	benign	catalyst
to be aggressive or show strong dislike	nonharmful, gentle	Something that quickly causes a change or action

EXTENDED READING

"Why Wolves Are Forever Wild and Dogs Can Be Tamed"
Discovery.com

"Dogs, But Not Wolves, Use Humans as Tools"
Jason G. Goldman
Scientific American, 2012

"How Werewolves Work"
How Stuff Works.com

Interview with Suzanne Stone
(Wolf Expert for Defenders of Wildlife)
Outdoor Idaho

"About the Wolves of Isle Royale Project"
Wolves and Moose of Isle Royale Website

READING CLOSELY
FOR TEXTUAL DETAILS

DEVELOPING CORE LITERACY PROFICIENCIES

GRADE 6

Literacy Toolbox

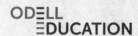

READING CLOSELY GRAPHIC

1.
APPROACHING
Where do I START?

- I determine my reading purposes and take note of important information about the text.

- Why am I reading this text, and how might that influence how I approach and read it?
- What do I know (or might find out) about the text's title, author, type, publisher, publication date, and history?
- **What sequence of questions might I use to focus my reading and increase my understanding of the text?**

2.
QUESTIONING
What details do I NOTICE?

- I use questions to help me investigate important aspects of the text.

3.
ANALYZING
What do I THINK about the details?

- I question further to analyze the details I notice and determine their meaning or importance.

4.
DEEPENING
How do I deepen my UNDERSTANDING?

- I consider others' questions and develop initial observations or claims.
- I explain why and cite my evidence.

5.
EXTENDING
Where does this LEAD me?

- I pose new questions to extend my investigation of the text and topic.
- I communicate my thinking to others.

ODELL
EDUCATION

READING CLOSELY: GUIDING QUESTIONS

1.
APPROACHING
Where do I START?

- I determine my reading purposes and take note of important information about the text.

- Why am I reading this text, and how might that influence how I approach and read it?
- What do I know (or might find out) about the text's title, author, type, publisher, publication date, and history?
- **What sequence of questions might I use to focus my reading and increase my understanding of the text?**

LANGUAGE (CCSS R.4, L.3, L.4, L.5)	IDEAS (CCSS R.2, W.3, R.8, R.9)	PERSPECTIVE (CCSS R.6)	STRUCTURE (CCSS R.5)
• What words or phrases stand out to me as powerful and important? • What do the author's words and phrases cause me to see, feel, or think? • How are key ideas, events, places, or characters described? • What unfamiliar words do I need to study or define to better understand the text?	• What do I think the text is mainly about—what is discussed in detail? • What new ideas or information do I find in the text? • Who are the main people, voices, or characters presented in the text? • What claims do I find in the text? • What ideas stand out to me as significant or interesting?	• What do I learn about the author and the purpose for writing the text? • What details or words suggest the author's perspective? • What seems to be the author's (narrator's) attitude or point of view?	• What do I notice about how the text is organized or sequenced? • What do I notice about the structure of specific elements (paragraphs, sentences, stanzas, lines, or scenes)? • In what ways does the text begin, end, and develop?
• How do specific words or phrases influence the meaning or tone of the text? • How does the author's choice of words reveal his or her purposes and perspective? • How does context define or change the meaning of key words in the text? • How does the text's language influence my understanding of important ideas or themes?	• How might I summarize the main ideas of the text and the key supporting details? • How do the text's main ideas relate to what I already know, think, or have read? • How do the main ideas, events, or people change as the text progresses? • What evidence supports the claims in the text, and what is left uncertain or unsupported?	• How does the author's perspective influence his or her presentation of ideas, themes, or arguments? • How does the author's perspective and presentation of the text compare to others? • How does the author's perspective influence my reading of the text?	• In what ways are ideas, events, and claims linked together in the text? • How do specific sections or elements of the text develop its central ideas or themes? • How does the organization of the text influence my understanding of its information, themes, or arguments?

2.
QUESTIONING
What details do I NOTICE?

- I use questions to help me investigate important aspects of the text.

3.
ANALYZING
What do I THINK about the details?

- I question further to analyze the details I notice and determine their meaning or importance.

- What relationships do I discover among the ideas and details presented, the author's perspective, and the language or structure of the text?

4.
DEEPENING
How do I deepen my UNDERSTANDING?

- I consider others' questions and develop initial observations or claims.
- I explain why and cite my evidence.

5.
EXTENDING
Where does this LEAD me?

- I pose new questions to extend my investigation of the text and topic.
- I communicate my thinking to others.

ODELL EDUCATION

ATTENDING TO DETAILS

SEARCHING FOR DETAILS	I read the text closely and mark words and phrases that help me answer my question.

As I read, I notice authors use a lot of details and strategies to develop their ideas, arguments and narratives. Below are examples of types of details authors often use in important ways.

SELECTING DETAILS	
I select words or phrases from my search that I think are important for answering my questions.	**Author's Facts and Ideas** • Statistics • Examples • Vivid description • Characters and actors • Events **Author's Language and Structure** • Repeated words • Strong language • Figurative language • Tone • Organizational structure and phrases **Opinions and Perspective** • Interpretations • Explanation of ideas or events • Narration • Personal reflection • Beliefs

By reading closely and thinking about the details, I can make connections among them. Below are some ways details can be connected.

ANALYZING DETAILS	
I reread parts of the text and think about the meaning of the details and what they tell me about my questions.	**Facts and Ideas** • Authors use hard facts to illustrate or define an idea. • Authors use examples to express a belief or point of view. • Authors use vivid description to compare or oppose different ideas. • Authors describe different actors or characters to illustrate a comparison or contrast. • Authors use a sequence of events to arrive at a conclusion. **Language and Structure** • Authors repeat specific words or structures to emphasize meaning or tone. • Authors use language or tone to establish a mood. • Authors use figurative language to infer emotion or embellish meaning. • Authors use a specific organization to enhance a point or add meaning. **Opinions and Perspective** • Authors compare or contrast evidence to help define their point of view. • Authors offer their explanation of ideas or events to support their beliefs. • Authors tell their own story to develop their point of view. • Authors use language to reveal an opinion or feeling about a topic.

ODELL EDUCATION

READING CLOSELY FINAL WRITING AND DISCUSSION TASK HANDOUT

In this unit, you have been developing your skills as an investigator of texts:

- Asking and thinking about good questions to help you examine what you read closely
- Uncovering key clues in the details, words, and information found in the texts
- Making connections among details and texts
- Discussing what you have discovered with your classmates and teacher
- Citing specific evidence from the texts to explain and support your thinking
- Recording and communicating your thinking on graphic tools and in sentences and paragraphs

Your final assignments will provide you with opportunities to use all of these related skills and to demonstrate your proficiency and growth in Reading Closely.

FINAL ASSIGNMENTS

1. **Becoming a Text Expert:** You will first become an expert about one of the three final texts in the unit. To accomplish this, you will do the following:
   a. Read and annotate the text on your own and use Guiding Questions and an ***Analyzing Details Tool*** to make some initial connections about the text.
   b. Compare the notes and connections you make with those made by other students who are also becoming experts about the same text.
   c. In your expert group, come up with a new text-specific question to think about when rereading the text more closely. Complete a second ***Analyzing Details Tool*** for this question.
   d. Study your text notes and ***Analyzing Details Tools*** to come up with your own central idea about the text and topic—something new you have come to understand.
   e. Think about how your text and the central idea you have discovered relates and compares to other texts in the unit.

2. **Writing a Text-Based Explanation:** On your own, you will plan and draft a multiparagraph explanation of something you have come to understand by reading and examining your text. To accomplish this, you will do the following:
   a. Present and explain the central idea you have found in the text—what you think the text is about.
   b. Use quotations and paraphrased references from the text to explain and support the central idea you are discussing.
   c. Explain how the central idea is related to what you have found out about the author's purpose in writing the text and the author's perspective on (view of) the topic.
   d. Present and explain a new understanding about the unit's topic that your text has led you to.
   e. Work with other students to review and improve your draft—and to be sure it is the best possible representation of your ideas and your skills as a reader and writer.
   f. Reflect on how well you have used Literacy Skills in developing this final explanation.

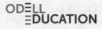

READING CLOSELY FINAL TASK HANDOUT (Continued)

FINAL ASSIGNMENTS (Continued)

3. **Leading and Participating in a Text-Centered Discussion:** After you have become an expert about your text and written an explanation of what you understand, you will prepare for and participate in a final discussion. In this discussion, you and other students will compare your close readings of the final three texts in the unit. To accomplish this, you will do the following:

   a. Prepare a summary of what you have come to understand and written in your explanation to share with the other students in your discussion group.

   b. Reread the other two final texts so that you are prepared to discuss and compare them.

   c. Meet with your expert group to talk about your text and how to lead a discussion of it.

   d. Come up with a new question about your text that will get others to think about the connections between it and the other texts in the unit.

   e. Join a new discussion group, and share your summary about your text and the evidence you have found:

      ⇒ Point out key details to the other students in your group.

      ⇒ Explain your observations about your author's purpose and perspective.

      ⇒ Point out key words, phrases, or sentences that indicate your author's perspective.

      ⇒ Explain what you have come to understand about the topic from your text.

   f. Listen to other students' summaries and think about the connections to your text.

   g. Pose your question to the group, and lead a discussion about the three texts, asking students to present evidence from the texts that supports their thinking.

   h. Reflect on how well you have used Discussion Habits in this final discussion.

SKILLS AND HABITS TO BE DEMONSTRATED

As you become a text expert, write your text-based explanation, and participate in a text-centered discussion, think about demonstrating the Literacy Skills and Discussion Habits listed in the following to the best of your ability. Your teacher will evaluate your work and determine your grade based on how well you do the following things:

- **Attend to Details:** Identify words, details, or quotations that you think are important to understanding the text.

- **Interpret Language:** Understand how words are used to express ideas and perspectives.

- **Summarize:** Correctly explain what the text says about the topic.

- **Identify Relationships:** Notice important connections among details, ideas, or texts.

- **Recognize Perspective:** Identify and explain the author's view of the text's topic.

- **Use Evidence:** Use well-chosen details from the text to support your explanation. Accurately paraphrase or quote what the author says in the text.

- **Prepare:** Read the text(s) closely and think about the questions to prepare for a text-centered discussion.

READING CLOSELY FINAL TASK HANDOUT (Continued)

SKILLS AND HABITS TO BE DEMONSTRATED (Continued)

- **Question:** Ask and respond to questions that help the discussion group understand and compare the texts.
- **Collaborate:** Pay attention to other participants while you participate in and lead a text-centered discussion.
- **Communicate Clearly:** Present your ideas and supporting evidence so others can understand them.

Note: These skills and habits are also listed on the ***Student Literacy Skills and Discussion Habits Checklist***, which you can use to assess your work and the work of other students.

QUESTIONING PATH TOOL

Text 1—Representations of Wolves

APPROACHING:
I determine my reading purposes and take note of key information about the text. I identify the LIPS domain(s) that will guide my initial reading.

I will initially focus on *ideas* and supporting details.

QUESTIONING: *I use Guiding Questions to help me investigate the text (from the Guiding Questions Handout).*

1. What details stand out to me as I examine this image? [I]

2. What do I think this image is mainly about? [I]

ANALYZING: *I question further to connect and analyze the details I find (from the Guiding Questions Handout).*

3. How do specific details help me understand what is being depicted in the image? [I]

DEEPENING: *I consider the questions of others.*

4. In Image Set 1, what do I think is happening? What specific details support my answer?

5. In Image Set 2, what do I think is happening? What do the details of Image Set 2 make me think or feel about wolves and their behavior? How do my reactions to the images and their details compare to my thoughts about Image Set 1?

6. In Image Set 3, what do I think is happening? In the second (lower) image, what do the position and stances of the wolves indicate? What do the details in the surrounding snow suggest?

7. What do the details of the two artistic works in Image Set 4 suggest about how artists see and depict wolves?

8. In the first (upper) image of Image Set 4, what does the look on the little girl's face suggest? The wolf's face is not visible, but what do I think the details of his face might show me?

9. In the final image of Image Set 4, how do the details of the artist's depiction of the wolf's face link to the words he includes in the graphic?

EXTENDING: *I pose my own questions.*

Example:
10. What connections or comparisons do I notice among the nine images of wolves?

ODELL
EDUCATION

QUESTIONING PATH TOOL

Text 2—"A Brief History of Wolves in the United States"(Model 1)

APPROACHING: *I determine my reading purposes and take note of key information about the text. I identify the LIPS domain(s) that will guide my initial reading.*	I will initially focus on *ideas* and supporting details.
QUESTIONING: *I use Guiding Questions to help me investigate the text (from the* ***Guiding Questions Handout****).*	1. What do I think the text is mainly about—what is discussed in detail? [I] 2. What new ideas or information do I find in the text? [I]
ANALYZING: *I question further to connect and analyze the details I find (from the* ***Guiding Questions Handout****).*	3. How do specific details help me understand the central ideas or themes of the text? [I]
DEEPENING: *I consider the questions of others.*	4. What details and examples are presented in paragraphs 3 and 4 to explain the ways in which Native American cultures "revered the wolf"? 5. What details and examples are presented in paragraphs 5 and 6 to explain the contrasting views of European settlers who had "fear of wolves"?
EXTENDING: *I pose my own questions.*	*Example:* 6. Which details in paragraphs 7 to 9 cause me to rethink the historical persecution of wolves in the United States?

QUESTIONING PATH TOOL
Text 3—*Two Wolves* Video

APPROACHING:
I determine my reading purposes and take note of key information about the text. I identify the LIPS domain(s) that will guide my initial reading.

I will initially focus on *ideas* and supporting details. I will think about this video as a text and how it compares to print texts.

QUESTIONING: *I use Guiding Questions to help me investigate the text (from the **Guiding Questions Handout**).*

1. What do I think the video is mainly about? [I]

ANALYZING: *I question further to connect and analyze the details I find (from the **Guiding Questions Handout**).*

2. How do specific details help me understand the central ideas or themes of the video and text? [I]

DEEPENING: *I consider the questions of others.*

3. What human qualities does the grandfather link to the "evil and ugly" wolf (1:50 into the video)? Why?

4. What human qualities does the grandfather link to the "beautiful and good" wolf (2:20 into the video)? Why?

5. How might I explain the grandfather's answer to the question: "Which wolf will win?"

EXTENDING: *I pose my own questions.*

Example:
6. How does the representation of the legend in the video connect or compare to the depiction in the two wolves graphic image (Text 1, Image Set 4)?

ODELL EDUCATION

QUESTIONING PATH TOOL

Independent Web Search

APPROACHING:
I determine my reading purposes and take note of key information about the text. I identify the LIPS domain(s) that will guide my initial reading.

I will focus on new *ideas* and information I can bring back to the class. I will note key information about the website I visit and its author or source.

QUESTIONING: *I use Guiding Questions to help me investigate the text (from the **Guiding Questions Handout**).*

1. What information or ideas are described or explained in detail? [I]

ANALYZING: *I question further to connect and analyze the details I find (from the **Guiding Questions Handout**).*

2. What key details and ideas would a summary of the website include? [I]

DEEPENING: *I consider the questions of others.*

3. What interesting details, examples, or ideas can I find that relate to the other texts we are studying?

EXTENDING: *I pose my own questions.*

Students might be asked to pose a question and bring back information related to their question.

APPROACHING TEXTS TOOL

Name _____   Text _____

APPROACHING THE TEXT

Before reading, I consider what my specific purposes for reading are.

What are my reading purposes?

_____
_____
_____

I also take note of key information about the text.

Title:	Author:	Source/Publisher:
	Text type:	Publication date:

What do I already think or understand about the text based on this information?

_____
_____

QUESTIONING THE TEXT

As I read the text for the first time, I use Guiding Questions that relate to my reading purpose and focus. (Can be taken from the Guiding Questions Handout.)

Guiding Questions for my first reading of the text:

_____
_____
_____

As I read I mark details on the text that relate to my Guiding Questions.

As I reread, I use questions I have about specific details that have emerged in my reading to focus my analysis and deepen my understanding.

Text-specific questions to help focus my rereading of the text:

_____
_____

ODELL EDUCATION

APPROACHING TEXTS TOOL

Name _____ Text _____

APPROACHING THE TEXT	What are my reading purposes?	
Before reading, I consider what my specific purposes for reading are.		
I also take note of key information about the text.	**Title:**	**Source/Publisher:**
	Text type:	**Publication date:**
	What do I already think or understand about the text based on this information?	

QUESTIONING THE TEXT	Guiding Questions for *my first reading* of the text:	
As I read the text for the first time, I use Guiding Questions that relate to my reading purpose and focus. (*Can be taken from the Guiding Questions Handout.*)		
	As I read I mark details on the text that relate to my Guiding Questions.	
As I reread, I use questions I have about specific details that have emerged in my reading to focus my analysis and deepen my understanding.	Text-specific questions to help focus *my rereading* of the text:	

ODELL
EDUCATION

QUESTIONING PATH TOOL

Text 2—"A Brief History of Wolves in the United States" (Model 2)

APPROACHING:
I determine my reading purposes and take note of key information about the text. I identify the LIPS domain(s) that will guide my initial reading.

I will examine *language* and its relationship to *ideas* and *perspective*. I will think about how knowing that the text comes from an advocacy group called Defenders of Wildlife might influence my rereading of it.

QUESTIONING: *I use Guiding Questions to help me investigate the text (from the **Guiding Questions Handout**).*

1. What words or phrases stand out to me as important? [L]

2. What unfamiliar words do I need to study or define to better understand the text? [L]

ANALYZING: *I question further to connect and analyze the details I find (from the **Guiding Questions Handout**).*

3. What details or words suggest the author's perspective? [P]

4. How does the author's choice of words reveal his or her purpose or perspective? [L]

DEEPENING: *I consider the questions of others.*

5. In paragraphs 5 to 9, what are the meanings of key words chosen by the author to discuss how wolves have been treated in the United States, for example, *legacy of persecution, scapegoat, extirpating*?

6. How do these words combine with key details (i.e., at the end of paragraph 7) to develop the ideas of the text and tell us something about how the author views the history of wolves in the United States?

EXTENDING: *I pose my own questions.*

Example:
7. What details does the author present to make me agree with her perspective? Disagree?

ODELL
EDUCATION

QUESTIONING PATH TOOL

Text 5—"All About Wolves": Hunting Behavior

APPROACHING:
I determine my reading purposes and take note of key information about the text. I identify the LIPS domain(s) that will guide my initial reading.

I will initially focus on the text's *ideas* and supporting details but will also pay attention to its *perspective* and *language*. I will think about how knowing the text comes from a website that documents a long-term scientific study of wolves might influence my reading.

QUESTIONING: *I use Guiding Questions to help me investigate the text (from the **Guiding Questions Handout**).*

1. What do I think the text is mainly about—what is discussed in detail? [I]

2. What new ideas or information do I find in the text? [I]

ANALYZING: *I question further to connect and analyze the details I find (from the **Guiding Questions Handout**).*

3. What do I learn about the authors and the purpose for writing the text? [P]

4. What details or words suggest the author's perspective? [P, L]

DEEPENING: *I consider the questions of others.*

5. In paragraphs 1 and 2, what do I discover about the authors, their relationship to the topic, and their purpose(s) for writing the text?

6. In paragraphs 3 to 6, which specific details explain how wolves work in packs to hunt moose? Which words and details suggest the authors' perspective about wolves' hunting behavior?

7. What do I learn about how wolves "consume . . . their prey?" Which words and details suggest the authors' perspective?

8. The authors claim that "in a fundamental way, wolves perceive a world that is simply beyond our comprehension." Which details in paragraphs 24 to 27 explain this claim, and how do they suggest the authors' perspective?

9. In paragraph 23, the authors claim that, "In some important ways, wolves, and humans are alike . . . In other ways, we differ."

   What details in "All About Wolves" suggest ways in which wolves and humans are similar? What details suggest ways in which wolves and humans are different?

10. In what ways do these opposing claims and their related details help me understand the authors' purpose and perspective?

EXTENDING: *I pose my own questions.*

Students might read paragraphs 30 to 36, looking at language and details, and then frame a question related to the life expectancy and social behavior of wolves. [Note: This extending activity can set the stage for a further extension when reading Text 6 in Part 3.]

APPROACHING TEXTS TOOL

Name _____   Text _____

APPROACHING THE TEXT	
Before reading, I consider what my specific purposes for reading are.	**What are my reading purposes?**
I also take note of key information about the text.	**Title:**	**Author:**
		Source/Publisher:
	Text type:	**Publication date:**
	What do I already think or understand about the text based on this information?	

QUESTIONING THE TEXT	
As I read the text for the first time, I use Guiding Questions that relate to my reading purpose and focus. (Can be taken from the Guiding Questions Handout.)	**Guiding Questions for my first reading of the text:**
	As I read I mark details on the text that relate to my Guiding Questions.
As I reread, I use questions I have about specific details that have emerged in my reading to focus my analysis and deepen my understanding.	**Text-specific questions to help focus my rereading of the text:**

ODELL
EDUCATION

ANALYZING DETAILS TOOL

Name _ _ _ _ _ _ _ _ _ _ _ _ _ _ **Text** _ _ _ _ _ _ _ _ _ _ _

Reading purpose:

A question I have about the text:

SEARCHING FOR DETAILS

I read the text closely and mark words and phrases that help me think about my question.

SELECTING DETAILS

I select words or phrases from my search that I think are the most important in thinking about my question.

Detail 1 (Ref.:)	Detail 2 (Ref.:)	Detail 3 (Ref.:)

ANALYZING DETAILS

I reread parts of the text and think about the meaning of the details and what they tell me about my question.

What I think about detail 1:	What I think about detail 2:	What I think about detail 3:

CONNECTING DETAILS

I compare the details and explain the connections I see among them.

How I connect the details:

ODELL EDUCATION

ANALYZING DETAILS TOOL

Name _____

Text _____

Reading purpose:

A question I have about the text:

SEARCHING FOR DETAILS	I read the text closely and mark words and phrases that help me think about my question.

SELECTING DETAILS	Detail 1 (Ref.:)	Detail 2 (Ref.:)	Detail 3 (Ref.:)
I select words or phrases from my search that I think are the most important in thinking about my question.			

ANALYZING DETAILS	What I think about detail 1:	What I think about detail 2:	What I think about detail 3:
I reread parts of the text and think about the meaning of the details and what they tell me about my question.			

CONNECTING DETAILS	How I connect the details:
I compare the details and explain the connections I see among them.	

ANALYZING DETAILS TOOL

Name _ _ _ _ _ _ _ _ _ _ _ _ _ _ _ _ _ _

Text _ _ _ _ _ _ _ _ _ _ _ _ _ _ _ _ _ _

Reading purpose:

A question I have about the text:

SEARCHING FOR DETAILS

I read the text closely and mark words and phrases that help me think about my question.

SELECTING DETAILS

I select words or phrases from my search that I think are the most important in thinking about my question.

Detail 1 (Ref.:)	Detail 2 (Ref.:)	Detail 3 (Ref.:)

ANALYZING DETAILS

I reread parts of the text and think about the meaning of the details and what they tell me about my question.

What I think about detail 1:	What I think about detail 2:	What I think about detail 3:

CONNECTING DETAILS

I compare the details and explain the connections I see among them.

How I connect the details:

ODELL EDUCATION

QUESTIONING PATH TOOL

Text 6—White Fang, "The Battle of the Fangs"

APPROACHING: *I determine my reading purposes and take note of key information about the text. I identify the LIPS domain(s) that will guide my initial reading.*

I will focus on the author's use of descriptive *language* and how it reveals his *perspective*. I will think about how the author, as a writer of fiction, may be using language to dramatize the characters and events he describes.

QUESTIONING: *I use Guiding Questions to help me investigate the text (from the **Guiding Questions Handout**).*

1. What do the author's words and phrases cause me to see, feel, or think? [L]

2. How are important events or characters described? [L]

ANALYZING: *I question further to connect and analyze the details I find (from the **Guiding Questions Handout**).*

3. How does the author's choice of words reveal his purpose or perspective? [L-P]

DEEPENING: *I consider the questions of others.*

4. In the first six paragraphs, what details are presented to describe each of the wolves in the pack:

   - The large grey wolf (P2)?

   - The she-wolf (P3)?

   - The one-eyed wolf (P4)?

   - The three-year-old (P5)?

   What do these details make us think about the pack and its behavior?

5. The author tells us that "the situation of the pack was desperate." What details in paragraphs 7 and 8 describe and help us feel the desperation of the wolves to find food?

6. What happens in paragraphs 9 and 10? What details cause us to see and feel the violence of the wolf hunt?

EXTENDING: *I pose my own questions.*

Examples:
7. Based on the details I have analyzed, what sense do I have about the wolf pack and its leaders? What might I predict will happen next in the text?

ODELL
EDUCATION

APPROACHING TEXTS TOOL

Name _____ Text _____

APPROACHING THE TEXT

Before reading, I consider what my specific purposes for reading are.	What are my reading purposes?
I also take note of key information about the text.	Title:	Author:	Source/Publisher:
		Text type:	Publication date:
	What do I already think or understand about the text based on this information?

QUESTIONING THE TEXT

As I read the text for the first time, I use Guiding Questions that relate to my reading purpose and focus. *(Can be taken from the Guiding Questions Handout.)*	Guiding Questions for *my first reading* of the text:
	As I read I mark details on the text that relate to my Guiding Questions.
As I reread, I use questions I have about specific details that have emerged in my reading to focus my analysis and deepen my understanding.	Text-specific questions to help focus *my rereading* of the text:

ANALYZING DETAILS TOOL

Name _ _ _ _ _ _ _ _ _ _ _ _ _ _ Text _ _ _ _ _ _ _ _

Reading purpose:

A question I have about the text:

SEARCHING FOR DETAILS	I read the text closely and mark words and phrases that help me think about my question.

SELECTING DETAILS I select words or phrases from my search that I think are the **most important** in thinking about my question.	Detail 1 (Ref.:)	Detail 2 (Ref.:)	Detail 3 (Ref.:)

ANALYZING DETAILS I reread parts of the text and think about the meaning of the details and what they tell me about my question.	What I think about detail 1:	What I think about detail 2:	What I think about detail 3:

CONNECTING DETAILS I compare the details and explain the connections I see among them.	How I connect the details:

ODELL
EDUCATION

ANALYZING DETAILS TOOL

Name _____   Text _____

Reading purpose:

A question I have about the text:

SEARCHING FOR DETAILS

I read the text closely and mark words and phrases that help me think about my question.

SELECTING DETAILS

I select words or phrases from my search that I think are the most important in thinking about my question.

Detail 1 (Ref.:	Detail 2 (Ref.:)	Detail 3 (Ref.:)

ANALYZING DETAILS

I reread parts of the text and think about the meaning of the details and what they tell me about my question.

What I think about detail 1:	What I think about detail 2:	What I think about detail 3:

CONNECTING DETAILS

I compare the details and explain the connections I see among them.

How I connect the details:

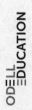

ODELL
EDUCATION

QUESTIONING PATH TOOL
Comparison of Text 5 and Text 6

APPROACHING: *I determine my reading purposes and take note of key information about the text. I identify the LIPS domain(s) that will guide my initial reading.*	I will compare the two texts' use of *language* and details to describe wolf behavior, and also how they reflect the author's *perspective(s)* as writers of nonfiction and fiction. Based on what I know about the two texts, I will think about the differences between informational and literary accounts.
QUESTIONING: *I use Guiding Questions to help me investigate the text (from the Guiding Questions Handout).*	1. What details or words suggest the author's perspective? [P-L]
ANALYZING: *I question further to connect and analyze the details I find (from the Guiding Questions Handout).*	2. How does the author's perspective influence the text's presentation of ideas, themes, or claims? [P] 3. How does the author's perspective and presentation of the text compare to others? [P]
DEEPENING: *I consider the questions of others.*	4. How does Jack London's (Text 6) description of the hunt (paragraphs 7 to 10) compare with the description in paragraphs 3 to 10 of "All About Wolves" (Text 5)? 5. In presenting a wolf's point of view, "All About Wolves" states that "communication and intelligence are needed to know who my friends and enemies are, where they are, and what may be their intentions." How does this observation relate to the details of the actions (and the wolf characters' thoughts) that are dramatized in Jack London's story? 6. Find another statement about wolf behavior from "All About Wolves." Connect this statement to something that is described in Jack London's depiction of the wolf pack. How are the two passages similar and different?
EXTENDING: *I pose my own questions.*	*Examples:* 7. What are the differences in my experiences as a reader as I read these two texts? 8. What aspects of the texts affect my different reading experiences?

ODELL
EDUCATION

ANALYZING DETAILS TOOL

Name - **Text** -

Reading purpose:

A question I have about the text:

SEARCHING FOR DETAILS | I read the text closely and mark words and phrases that help me think about my question.

SELECTING DETAILS

I select words or phrases from my search that I think are the most important in thinking about my question.

Detail 1 (Ref.:)	Detail 2 (Ref.:)	Detail 3 (Ref.:)

ANALYZING DETAILS

I reread parts of the text and think about the meaning of the details and what they tell me about my question.

What I think about detail 1:	What I think about detail 2:	What I think about detail 3:

CONNECTING DETAILS

I compare the details and explain the connections I see among them.

How I connect the details:

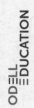

ODELL
EDUCATION

ANALYZING DETAILS TOOL

Name _ _ _ _ _ _ _ _ _ _ Text _ _ _ _ _ _ _ _ _ _ _ _ _

Reading purpose:

A question I have about the text:

SEARCHING FOR DETAILS — I read the text closely and mark words and phrases that help me think about my question.

Detail 1 (Ref.:)	Detail 2 (Ref.:)	Detail 3 (Ref.:)

SELECTING DETAILS

I select words or phrases from my search that I think are the most important in thinking about my question.

ANALYZING DETAILS —

What I think about detail 1:	What I think about detail 2:	What I think about detail 3:

I reread parts of the text and think about the meaning of the details and what they tell me about my question.

CONNECTING DETAILS — How I connect the details:

I compare the details and explain the connections I see among them.

ODELL
EDUCATION

QUESTIONING PATH: TEXTS 7, 8, AND 9

APPROACHING: *I determine my reading purposes and approach. I take note of key information about the text.*

I will do a first reading of the text, thinking about its author's purpose and *perspective*, its use of *language*, its new information and *ideas*, and how its themes are presented through text *structure*.

QUESTIONING: *I use Guiding Questions to help me investigate the text.*

1. What do I learn about the author and the purpose for writing the text? [P]

2. How are key ideas, events, places, or characters described? [L]

3. How do the text's main ideas relate to what I already know, think, or have read? [I]

4. How do specific sections or elements of the text develop its central ideas or themes? [S]

ANALYZING: *I question further to connect and analyze the details I find (from the **Guiding Questions Handout**).*

DEEPENING: *I consider the questions of others.*

EXTENDING: *I pose my own questions.*

APPROACHING TEXTS TOOL

Name _____   **Text** _____

APPROACHING THE TEXT	
Before reading, I consider what my specific purposes for reading are.	**What are my reading purposes?**
I also take note of key information about the text.	**Title:** **Author:** **Source/Publisher:** **Text type:** **Publication date:** **What do I already think or understand about the text based on this information?**

QUESTIONING THE TEXT	
As I read the text for the first time, I use Guiding Questions that relate to my reading purpose and focus. (Can be taken from the Guiding Questions Handout.)	**Guiding Questions for my first reading of the text:**
	As I read I mark details on the text that relate to my Guiding Questions.
As I reread, I use questions I have about specific details that have emerged in my reading to focus my analysis and deepen my understanding.	**Text-specific questions to help focus my rereading of the text:**

QUESTIONING PATH TOOL

Text 7—"All About Wolves": Pack Behavior

APPROACHING: *I determine my reading purposes and take note of key information about the text. I identify the LIPS domain(s) that will guide my initial reading.*

I will do a close reading of my text, looking for key details related to its *ideas, language, perspective,* or *structure,* in preparation for writing a text-based explanation and leading a comparative discussion. I will think about how the text comes from a source that presents both research about and advocacy for wolves.

QUESTIONING: *I use Guiding Questions to help me investigate the text (from the **Guiding Questions Handout**).*

1. What do I learn about the author (source) and the purpose for writing the text? [P]

2. How are key ideas, events, places, or characters described? [L]

ANALYZING: *I question further to connect and analyze the details I find (from the **Guiding Questions Handout**).*

3. How do the text's main ideas relate to what I already know, think, or have read? [I]

4. How do specific sections or elements of the text develop its central ideas or themes? [S]

DEEPENING: *I consider the questions of others.*

5. What is the author's purpose for writing this explanation on the Isle Royale website?

6. In the first four paragraphs of the "Observations of Pack Behavior," what important details do we learn about Isle Royale wolf pups in their first year of life?

7. What specific details are included about how wolves live in packs "in a complex web of social relationships" (P5–P8, P18)?

8. What specific details are included about wolf communication (P13–P15)?

9. In paragraph 21, the authors make a claim that "wolves are like humans." What details in the text support this claim?

10. After reading Texts 5 and 7, what picture of the life of Isle Royale wolves emerges? In what ways is it difficult? In what ways is it similar to or different from human life?

11. As presented in this text, do wolves seem more like the "good wolf" or the "bad wolf" from the Cherokee story? What details from the text support your answer?

EXTENDING: *I pose my own questions.*

Students will develop an original question for their text in Part 4 and a comparative question in Part 5.

QUESTIONING PATH TOOL

Text 8—*White Fang*, "The Grey Cub"

APPROACHING: *I determine my reading purposes and take note of key information about the text. I identify the LIPS domain(s) that will guide my initial reading.*	I will do a close reading of my text, looking for key details related to its *ideas, language, perspective,* or *structure,* in preparation for writing a text-based explanation and leading a comparative discussion. I will think about how this is a work of fiction.
QUESTIONING: *I use Guiding Questions to help me investigate the text (from the **Guiding Questions Handout**).*	1. What do I learn about the author and the purpose for writing the text? [P] 2. How are key ideas, events, places, or characters described? [L]
ANALYZING: *I question further to connect and analyze the details I find (from the **Guiding Questions Handout**).*	3. How do the text's main ideas relate to what I already know, think, or have read? [I] 4. How do specific sections or elements of the text develop its central ideas or themes? [S]
DEEPENING: *I consider the questions of others.*	5. What picture of the life of a young wolf pup does Jack London present? What might he want his readers to see or feel about wolf pups? 6. What details do we learn about the first few months of a wolf pup's life? 7. How do these details relate to information presented in the other informational texts? 8. How do the two Jack London excerpts, Texts 6 and 8, contrast in the picture they present of the life of the she-wolf, One Eye, and the pups? 9. What do we learn happens to One-Eye at the end of Text 8? How is this event surprising given what happens in the "battle of the fangs" in Text 6? 10. As presented in this text, do wolves seem more like the "good wolf" or the "bad wolf" from the Cherokee story? What details from the text support your answer?
EXTENDING: *I pose my own questions.*	*Students will develop an original question for their text in Part 4 and a comparative question in Part 5.*

ODELL
EDUCATION

QUESTIONING PATH TOOL

Text 9—"We Didn't Domesticate Dogs. They Domesticated Us."

APPROACHING:
I determine my reading purposes and take note of key information about the text. I identify the LIPS domain(s) that will guide my initial reading.

I will do a close reading of my text, looking for key details related to its *ideas, language, perspective,* or *structure,* in preparation for writing a text-based explanation and leading a comparative discussion. I will think about how the text is written by scientists who are proposing a new theory about wolves and dogs.

QUESTIONING: *I use Guiding Questions to help me investigate the text (from the **Guiding Questions Handout**).*

1. What do I learn about the author and the purpose for writing the text? [P]

2. How are key ideas, events, places, or characters described? [L]

ANALYZING: *I question further to connect and analyze the details I find (from the **Guiding Questions Handout**).*

3. How do the text's main ideas relate to what I already know, think, or have read? [I]

4. How do specific sections or elements of the text develop its central ideas or themes? [S]

DEEPENING: *I consider the questions of others.*

5. In the first four paragraphs, what evidence do the authors present for their claim that the "common assumption" about how wolves evolved into dogs "doesn't really make sense"?

6. What contrasting theory do the authors present about how wolves became dogs, and what details do they use to explain their ideas about "survival of the friendliest"?

7. What important ability do the authors suggest the "protodogs" developed, and what examples do they give about how this ability has been important for both dogs and humans?

8. In what ways does this article make us think differently about wolves than other texts in the unit? In what ways is its theory about wolves and dogs connected to information from other texts?

9. As presented in this text, do wolves seem more like the "good wolf" or the "bad wolf" from the Cherokee story? What details from the text support your answer?

EXTENDING: *I pose my own questions.*

Students will develop an original question for their text in Part 4 and a comparative question in Part 5.

APPROACHING TEXTS TOOL

Name _____ Text _____

APPROACHING THE TEXT	
Before reading, I consider what my specific purposes for reading are.	**What are my reading purposes?**
I also take note of key information about the text.	**Title:** **Author:**
	Text type: **Source/Publisher:**
	Publication date:
	What do I already think or understand about the text based on this information?

QUESTIONING THE TEXT	
As I read the text for the first time, I use Guiding Questions that relate to my reading purpose and focus. (*Can be taken from the Guiding Questions Handout.*)	**Guiding Questions for *my first reading* of the text:**
	As I read I mark details on the text that relate to my Guiding Questions.
As I reread, I use questions I have about specific details that have emerged in my reading to focus my analysis and deepen my understanding.	**Text-specific questions to help focus *my rereading* of the text:**

ODELL EDUCATION

ANALYZING DETAILS TOOL

Name _____ Text _ _ _ _ _ _ _ _ _ _ _ _

Reading purpose:

A question I have about the text:

SEARCHING FOR DETAILS

I read the text closely and mark words and phrases that help me think about my question.

SELECTING DETAILS

I select words or phrases from my search that I think are the most important in thinking about my question.

Detail 1 (Ref.:)	Detail 2 (Ref.:)	Detail 3 (Ref.:)

ANALYZING DETAILS

I reread parts of the text and think about the meaning of the details and what they tell me about my question.

What I think about detail 1:	What I think about detail 2:	What I think about detail 3:

CONNECTING DETAILS

I compare the details and explain the connections I see among them.

How I connect the details:

ANALYZING DETAILS TOOL

Name _____ Text _____

Reading purpose:

A question I have about the text:

SEARCHING FOR DETAILS	I read the text closely and mark words and phrases that help me think about my question.		
SELECTING DETAILS I select words or phrases from my search that I think are the most important in thinking about my question.	Detail 1 (Ref.:)	Detail 2 (Ref.:)	Detail 3 (Ref.:)
ANALYZING DETAILS I reread parts of the text and think about the meaning of the details and what they tell me about my question.	What I think about detail 1:	What I think about detail 2:	What I think about detail 3:
CONNECTING DETAILS I compare the details and explain the connections I see among them.	How I connect the details:		

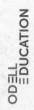
ODELL EDUCATION

ANALYZING DETAILS TOOL

Name _ _ _ _ _ _ _ _ _ _ _ _ | Text _ _ _ _ _ _ _ _ _ _ _ _ _ _ _ _ _ _

Reading purpose:

A question I have about the text:

SEARCHING FOR DETAILS	I read the text closely and mark words and phrases that help me think about my question.
SELECTING DETAILS I select words or phrases from my search that I think are the most important in thinking about my question.	Detail 1 (Ref.:) Detail 2 (Ref.:) Detail 3 (Ref.:)
ANALYZING DETAILS I reread parts of the text and think about the meaning of the details and what they tell me about my question.	What I think about detail 1: What I think about detail 2: What I think about detail 3:
CONNECTING DETAILS I compare the details and explain the connections I see among them.	How I connect the details:

ODELL
EDUCATION

PART 4: TEXT-BASED EXPLANATION LITERACY SKILLS CHECKLIST

LITERACY SKILLS	DESCRIPTORS: *Find evidence of using the literacy skill in the draft.* *Does the writer's explanation . . .*	NEEDS WORK	OKAY	VERY STRONG
ATTENDING TO DETAILS	Identify words, details, or quotations that are important to understanding the text?			
SUMMARIZING	Correctly explain what the text says about the topic?			
IDENTIFYING RELATIONSHIPS	Notice important connections among details, ideas, or texts?			
RECOGNIZING PERSPECTIVE	Identify and explain the author's view of the text's topic?			
USING EVIDENCE	Support the explanation with evidence from the text; use accurate quotations, paraphrases, and references?			

ODELL
EDUCATION

PART 5: TEXT-CENTERED DISCUSSION ACADEMIC HABITS CHECKLIST

DISCUSSION HABITS	DESCRIPTORS: *When—and how well—have I demonstrated these habits?*	EXAMPLES FROM *TEXT-CENTERED DISCUSSIONS*
PREPARING	Reads the text(s) closely and thinks about the questions to prepare for a text-centered discussion	
COLLABORATING	Pays attention to other participants while participating in and leading a text-centered discussion	
COMMUNICATING CLEARLY	Presents ideas and supporting evidence so others can understand them	

STUDENT READING CLOSELY LITERACY SKILLS AND DISCUSSION HABITS CHECKLIST

	READING CLOSELY LITERACY SKILLS AND DISCUSSION HABITS	✔	Evidence Demonstrating the Skills and Habits
READING AND THINKING	1. **Attending to Details:** Identifies words, details, or quotations that are important to understanding the text		
	2. **Interpreting Language:** Understands how words are used to express ideas and perspectives		
	3. **Summarizing:** Correctly explains what the text says about the topic		
	4. **Identifying Relationships:** Notices important connections among details, ideas, or texts		
	5. **Recognizing Perspective:** Identifies and explains the author's view of the text's topic		
	6. **Using Evidence:** Uses well-chosen details from the text to support explanations; accurately paraphrases or quotes		
DISCUSSION	7. **Preparing:** Reads the text(s) closely and thinks about the questions to prepare for a text-centered discussion		
	8. **Questioning:** Asks and responds to questions that help the discussion group understand and compare the texts		
	9. **Collaborating:** Pays attention to other participants while participating in and leading a text-centered discussion		
	10. **Communicating Clearly:** Presents ideas and supporting evidence so others can understand them		
	General comments:		

ODELL EDUCATION

MAKING
EVIDENCE-BASED CLAIMS

DEVELOPING CORE LITERACY
PROFICIENCIES

GRADE 6

"Connecting the Dots"
2005 Commencement Address
Stanford University
Steve Jobs

GOAL

In this unit you will develop your proficiency as a maker and defender of claims. You will learn how to do the following:

1. Use the details, connections, and evidence you find in a text to form a claim—a stated conclusion—about something you have discovered.
2. Organize evidence from the text to support your claim and make your case.
3. Express and explain your claim in writing.
4. Improve your writing so that others will clearly understand and appreciate your evidence-based claim—and think about the case you have made for it.

TOPIC

In this unit you will be reading and listening to a speech by Steve Jobs presented in 2005 to the graduating class at Stanford University. Jobs's speech will use stories from his life to communicate his message to the graduates. You will be learning about what a *claim* is and noting how the speaker makes claims that are based in the details of his own experience. As you apply the skills from *Reading Closely for Details* of finding key details and making connections, you will take the next step as a reader and thinker: forming your own claims that come from your reading of the text and supporting them with evidence that comes from what Steve Jobs says.

ACTIVITIES

As you move through this unit from initial reading to thinking, and to writing, the activities will help you do a close reading of short sections of the speech and to move from what Steve Jobs tells the graduates to what he seems to mean when you "read between the lines." You will first practice finding evidence from the speech to support a claim made by your teacher, then move on to forming your own first claims from details you notice in the text. You will continue to search for evidence that leads to and supports new claims and learn how to organize that evidence. From this base, you will write and revise several claims, the final one a global claim about the overall meaning you have found in the speech. You will learn to work with other students in the class to review and improve your writing so that your final claim can be as clear, strong, and evidence-based as possible.

MAKING EVIDENCE-BASED CLAIMS LITERACY TOOLBOX

In *Making Evidence-Based Claims*, you will continue to build your "literacy toolbox" by learning how to use the following handouts, tools and checklists organized in your Student Edition.

TOOLS

In *Making Evidence-Based Claims,* you will learn how to use the following tools organized in your Student Edition. You will also apply tools from *Reading Closely*:

Approaching the Text Tool

from the *Reading Closely* unit

Analyzing Details Tool

from the *Reading Closely* unit

Questioning Path Tool

from the *Reading Closely* unit

Model Questioning Paths

For each section of the text you will read, there is a *Questioning Path Tool* that has been filled out for you to frame and guide your reading. These model Questioning Paths are just starting points, and your teacher or you may prefer to develop your own paths. The model paths are organized by the steps from the *Reading Closely Graphic* (approaching, questioning, analyzing, deepening, and extending). They include general Guiding Questions from the *Guiding Questions Handout* and some questions that are specific to each text and its content. You will use these model paths to guide your reading, frame your discussions with your teacher and other students, and help you when you are doing the final activities in the unit.

Forming Evidence-Based Claims Tool

This three-part tool will help you move in your thinking from *finding* important details, to *connecting* those details and explaining your connections, to *making a claim* based on the details and connections you have found. You can also use the tool to record evidence to support your claim and indicate where in the text you found the evidence.

Supporting Evidence-Based Claims Tool

This tool provides spaces in which you can record one or more claims about the text (either your teacher's or your own) and then quote or paraphrase supporting evidence for the claim(s)—which you will later use in organizing and writing your claim.

Organizing Evidence-Based Claims Tool

This tool provides support as you move from forming a claim and finding supporting evidence to writing the claim. The tool provides space for writing down two or three supporting points you will want to make to explain and prove your claim. Under each of these points, you can then organize the evidence you have found that relates to the point and supports your overall claim.

HANDOUTS

To support your work with the texts and the tools, you will be able to use the following informational handouts:

Attending to Details Handout

from the *Reading Closely* unit

Guiding Questions Handout

from the *Reading Closely* unit

Writing Evidence-Based Claims Handout

This handout explains five key things you will need to think about as you write an evidence-based claim. These characteristics are also things your teacher will be looking for in the final claim you write and turn in. The handout includes examples related to Steve Jobs's speech so you can see what each of the key characteristics might look like.

Final Writing Tasks

This handout will explain to you what you will be doing in the final assignments for this unit: writing a paragraph that elaborates a claim about the final section of the text and writing a multiparagraph essay that presents, explains, and uses evidence to support a claim you have formed about the meaning of Steve Jobs's speech. The handout will also help you know what your teacher will be looking for so you can be successful on the essay assignment.

CHECKLISTS

You will also use these checklists throughout the unit to support peer- and self-review:

Making Evidence-Based Claims Skills and Habits Checklists

These two checklists present and briefly describe the Literacy Skills and Habits you will be working on during the unit. You can use the checklists to remind you of what you are trying to learn; to reflect on what you have done when reading, discussing, or writing; or to give feedback to other students. Your teacher may use them to let you know about your areas of strength and areas in which you can improve.

Self- and Peer-Review Checklists

These checklists highlight key activities such as discussions, developing claims, and writing essays. The checklists can help you think about how well you are doing on the habits and skills these activities involve.

MAKING EVIDENCE-BASED CLAIMS UNIT TEXT

Stanford University Commencement Address
Steve Jobs
June 12, 2005

I am honored to be with you today at your **commencement** from one of the finest universities in the **P1**
world. I never graduated from college. Truth be told, this is the closest I've ever gotten to a college
graduation. Today I want to tell you three stories from my life. That's it. No big deal. Just three stories.

The first story is about connecting the dots. **P2**

5 I dropped out of Reed College after the first six months, but then stayed around as a drop-in for **P3**
another eighteen months or so before I really quit. So why did I drop out?

It started before I was born. My biological mother was a young, unwed college graduate student, **P4**
and she decided to put me up for adoption. She felt very strongly that I should be adopted by college
graduates, so everything was all set for me to be adopted at birth by a lawyer and his wife. Except that
10 when I popped out they decided at the last minute that they really wanted a girl. So my parents, who
were on a waiting list, got a call in the middle of the night asking: "We have an unexpected baby boy;
do you want him?" They said: "Of course." My biological mother later found out that my mother had
never graduated from college and that my father had never graduated from high school. She refused
to sign the final adoption papers. She only **relented** a few months later when my parents promised
15 that I would someday go to college.

commencement	relented	
graduation, in this case from a university	gave in; yielded	

And 17 years later I did go to college. But I **naively** chose a college that was almost as expensive as P5 Stanford, and all of my working-class parents' savings were being spent on my college tuition. After six months, I couldn't see the value in it. I had no idea what I wanted to do with my life and no idea how college was going to help me figure it out. And here I was spending all of the money my parents

20 had saved their entire life. So I decided to drop out and trust that it would all work out OK. It was pretty scary at the time, but looking back it was one of the best decisions I ever made. The minute I dropped out I could stop taking the required classes that didn't interest me, and begin dropping in on the ones that looked interesting.

It wasn't all romantic. I didn't have a dorm room, so I slept on the floor in friends' rooms, I returned P6

25 coke bottles for the five-cent deposits to buy food with, and I would walk the seven miles across town every Sunday night to get one good meal a week at the Hare Krishna temple. I loved it. And much of what I stumbled into by following my curiosity and intuition turned out to be priceless later on. Let me give you one example: Reed College at that time offered perhaps the best **calligraphy** instruction in the country. Throughout the campus every poster, every label on every drawer, was beautifully

30 hand calligraphed. Because I had dropped out and didn't have to take the normal classes, I decided to take a calligraphy class to learn how to do this. I learned about **serif and san serif typefaces**, about varying the amount of space between different letter combinations, about what makes great **typography** great. It was beautiful, historical, artistically subtle in a way that science can't capture, and I found it fascinating.

35 None of this had even a hope of any practical application in my life. But ten years later, when we were P7 designing the first Macintosh computer, it all came back to me. And we designed it all into the Mac.

naively	calligraphy	serif typeface
innocently and unwisely	the art of producing decorative handwritten lettering with a pen or brush	style of typeface with decorative lines on the letters (e.g., Times)
san serif typeface	**typography**	
style of typeface with simple lines (e.g., Arial)	the style and appearance of printed matter; the art of arranging	

Developing Core Literacy Proficiencies

It was the first computer with beautiful typography. If I had never dropped in on that single course in college, the Mac would have never had multiple typefaces or proportionally spaced fonts. And since Windows just copied the Mac, it's likely that no personal computer would have them. If I had never dropped out, I would have never dropped in on this calligraphy class, and personal computers might not have the wonderful typography that they do. Of course it was impossible to connect the dots looking forward when I was in college. But it was very, very clear looking backwards ten years later.

Again, you can't connect the dots looking forward; you can only connect them looking backwards. **P8** So you have to trust that the dots will somehow connect in your future. You have to trust in something—your gut, destiny, life, **karma**, whatever. This approach has never let me down, and it has made all the difference in my life.

My second story is about love and loss. **P9**

I was lucky—I found what I loved to do early in life. Woz and I started Apple in my parents' garage **P10** when I was twenty. We worked hard, and in ten years Apple had grown from just the two of us in a garage into a two-billion-dollar company with over four thousand employees. We had just released our finest creation—the Macintosh—a year earlier, and I had just turned thirty. And then I got fired. How can you get fired from a company you started? Well, as Apple grew we hired someone who I thought was very talented to run the company with me, and for the first year or so things went well. But then our visions of the future began to **diverge** and eventually we had a falling out. When we did, our Board of Directors sided with him. So at thirty I was out. And very publicly out. What had been the focus of my entire adult life was gone, and it was devastating.

I really didn't know what to do for a few months. I felt that I had let the previous generation of **P11** **entrepreneurs** down—that I had dropped the baton as it was being passed to me. I met with David

karma	diverge	entrepreneur
good or bad luck, seen as resulting from one's actions (from Hinduism and Buddhism)	differ; move away from each other	a person who sets up a business, taking on financial risks to make

Packard and Bob Noyce and tried to apologize for screwing up so badly. I was a very public failure, and

60 I even thought about running away from the valley. But something slowly began to dawn on me—I still loved what I did. The turn of events at Apple had not changed that one bit. I had been rejected, but I was still in love. And so I decided to start over.

I didn't see it then, but it turned out that getting fired from Apple was the best thing that could have   **P12**
ever happened to me. The heaviness of being successful was replaced by the lightness of being a

65 beginner again, less sure about everything. It freed me to enter one of the most creative periods of my life.

During the next five years, I started a company named NeXT, another company named Pixar, and fell   **P13**
in love with an amazing woman who would become my wife. Pixar went on to create the world's first computer animated feature film, *Toy Story,* and is now the most successful animation studio in the

70 world. In a remarkable turn of events, Apple bought NeXT, I returned to Apple, and the technology we developed at NeXT is at the heart of Apple's current **renaissance.** And Laurene and I have a wonderful family together.

I'm pretty sure none of this would have happened if I hadn't been fired from Apple. It was awful   **P14**
tasting medicine, but I guess the patient needed it. Sometimes life hits you in the head with a brick.

75 Don't lose faith. I'm convinced that the only thing that kept me going was that I loved what I did. You've got to find what you love. And that is as true for your work as it is for your lovers. Your work is going to fill a large part of your life, and the only way to be truly satisfied is to do what you believe is great work. And the only way to do great work is to love what you do. If you haven't found it yet, keep looking. Don't settle. As with all matters of the heart, you'll know when you find it. And, like any

80 great relationship, it just gets better and better as the years roll on. So keep looking until you find it. Don't settle.

renaissance		
a revival or renewed interest in something		

My third story is about death. P15

When I was seventeen, I read a quote that went something like: "If you live each day as if it was your P16 last, someday you'll most certainly be right." It made an impression on me, and since then, for the past

85 33 years, I have looked in the mirror every morning and asked myself: "If today were the last day of my life, would I want to do what I am about to do today?" And whenever the answer has been "No" for too many days in a row, I know I need to change something.

Remembering that I'll be dead soon is the most important tool I've ever encountered to help me P17 make the big choices in life. Because almost everything—all external expectations, all pride, all fear of

90 embarrassment or failure—these things just fall away in the face of death, leaving only what is truly important. Remembering that you are going to die is the best way I know to avoid the trap of thinking you have something to lose. You are already naked. There is no reason not to follow your heart.

About a year ago I was diagnosed with cancer. I had a scan at 7:30 in the morning, and it clearly P18 showed a tumor on my **pancreas**. I didn't even know what a pancreas was. The doctors told me this

95 was almost certainly a type of cancer that is incurable, and that I should expect to live no longer than three to six months. My doctor advised me to go home and get my affairs in order, which is doctor's code for prepare to die. It means to try to tell your kids everything you thought you'd have the next 10 years to tell them in just a few months. It means to make sure everything is buttoned up so that it will be as easy as possible for your family. It means to say your goodbyes.

100 I lived with that diagnosis all day. Later that evening I had a **biopsy**, where they stuck an **endoscope** P19 down my throat, through my stomach and into my intestines, put a needle into my pancreas and got

pancreas	biopsy	endoscope
a large gland behind the stomach which aids in digestion (and can be affected by cancer)	an examination of body tissue to discover the presence or cause of disease	an instrument used to give a view of the body's internal parts

a few cells from the tumor. I was sedated, but my wife, who was there, told me that when they viewed the cells under a microscope the doctors started crying because it turned out to be a very rare form of pancreatic cancer that is curable with surgery. I had the surgery and I'm fine now.

105 This was the closest I've been to facing death, and I hope it's the closest I get for a few more decades. **P20** Having lived through it, I can now say this to you with a bit more certainty than when death was a useful but purely intellectual concept:

No one wants to die. Even people who want to go to heaven don't want to die to get there. And yet **P21** death is the destination we all share. No one has ever escaped it. And that is as it should be, because
110 Death is very likely the single best invention of Life. It is Life's change agent. It clears out the old to make way for the new. Right now the new is you, but someday not too long from now, you will gradually become the old and be cleared away. Sorry to be so dramatic, but it is quite true.

Your time is limited, so don't waste it living someone else's life. Don't be trapped by **dogma**—which **P22** is living with the results of other people's thinking. Don't let the noise of others' opinions drown out
115 your own inner voice. And most important, have the courage to follow your heart and **intuition.** They somehow already know what you truly want to become. Everything else is secondary.

When I was young, there was an amazing publication called *The Whole Earth Catalog,* which was one **P23** of the bibles of my generation. It was created by a fellow named Stewart Brand not far from here in Menlo Park, and he brought it to life with his poetic touch. This was in the late 1960s, before personal
120 computers and desktop publishing, so it was all made with typewriters, scissors, and polaroid cameras. It was sort of like Google in paperback form, 35 years before Google came along: it was **idealistic**, and overflowing with neat tools and great notions.

dogma	intuition	idealistic
a principle or idea presented by an authority as unarguably true	the ability to understand something immediately and instinctively	aiming or hoping for perfection, sometimes unrealistically

Developing Core Literacy Proficiencies

Stewart and his team put out several issues of *The Whole Earth Catalog*, and then when it had run   P24
its course, they put out a final issue. It was the mid-1970s, and I was your age. On the back cover of
125 their final issue was a photograph of an early morning country road, the kind you might find yourself
hitchhiking on if you were so adventurous. Beneath it were the words: "Stay Hungry. Stay Foolish." It
was their farewell message as they signed off. Stay Hungry. Stay Foolish. And I have always wished
that for myself. And now, as you graduate to begin anew, I wish that for you.

Stay Hungry. Stay Foolish.   P25

Thank you all very much.   P26

MAKING EVIDENCE-BASED CLAIMS

DEVELOPING CORE LITERACY PROFICIENCIES

GRADE 6

Literacy Toolbox

WRITING EVIDENCE-BASED CLAIMS

Writing evidence-based claims is a little different from writing stories or just writing about something. You need to follow a few steps as you write.

1. ESTABLISH THE CONTEXT

Your readers must know **where your claim is coming from** and **why it's important.**

Depending on the scope of your piece and the claim, the context differs. If your whole piece is one claim or if you're introducing the first major claim of your piece, the entire context must be given:

> In his speech to Stanford graduates in 2005, Steve Jobs tells a story. . .

Purposes of evidence-based writing vary. In some cases, naming the article and author is enough to show why your claim is important. In other cases, you might want to give more information:

> Steve Jobs led an inspirational life. In his speech to Stanford graduates in 2005, Steve Jobs tells a story. . .

If your claim is part of a larger piece with multiple claims, then the context might be simpler:

> According to Jobs,. . .   *or*   In paragraph 5, Jobs claims…

2. STATE YOUR CLAIM CLEARLY

How you state your claim is important; it must **clearly and fully express your ideas.**

Figuring out how to state claims is a process. Writers revise them continually as they write their supporting evidence. Here's a claim about Jobs' speech:

> In his speech to Stanford graduates in 2005, Steve Jobs tells a story "about death" because he wants the graduates to realize something he has learned from having cancer: that Death is a necessary part of Life, which should influence how people live.

Remember, you should continually return and rephrase your claim as you write the supporting evidence to make sure you are capturing exactly what you want to say. Writing out the evidence always helps you figure out what you really think.

3. ORGANIZE YOUR SUPPORTING EVIDENCE

Most claims contain multiple parts that require different evidence and should be expressed in separate paragraphs. This claim can be **broken down into two parts:**

A description of how **Having cancer caused Jobs to face death**

and

how Jobs thinks death should shape how people live.

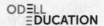

WRITING EVIDENCE-BASED CLAIMS (Continued)

3. ORGANIZE YOUR SUPPORTING EVIDENCE (Continued)

Here are two paragraphs that support the claim with evidence organized into these two parts.

A description of how Having cancer caused Jobs to face death:

> In his speech to Stanford graduates in 2005, Steve Jobs tells a story "about death" because he wants the graduates to realize something he has learned from having cancer: that Death is a necessary part of Life, which should influence how people live. When Jobs was first diagnosed with pancreatic cancer, he was told that it was incurable and that he would not live long (P18). Knowing he might die from cancer caused him to remember something he had thought since he was 17, that he should live every day as if it were his last (P17).

A description of the Jobs thinks death should shape how people live:

> In paragraph 5, Jobs introduces his message and tells the graduates that he can state his ideas "with a bit more certainty than when death was a useful but purely intellectual concept." In paragraph 21, he states several claims that explain how he now views death. He describes Death as "the single best invention of life" and "life's change agent" because it "clears out the old to make way for the new" (P21). Jobs's story about his cancer explains something he has said earlier in paragraph 17: "Remembering that I'll be dead soon is the most important tool I've ever encountered to help me make the big choices in life." Steve Jobs is telling the graduates that they should live their lives in a meaningful way, because, like him, they never know when life might end.

Notice the phrase, "In paragraph 20, Jobs introduces his message" starting the second paragraph. **Transitional phrases** like such as this one aid the organization by showing how the ideas relate to each other.

4. PARAPHRASE AND QUOTE

Written evidence from texts can be paraphrased or quoted. It's up to the writer to decide which works better for each piece of evidence. Paraphrasing is **putting the author's words into your own.** This works well when the author originally expresses the idea you want to include across many sentences. You might write it more briefly. The second line from the first paragraph paraphrases the evidence from Jobs's text. The ideas are his, but the exact way of writing is not.

> When Jobs was first diagnosed with pancreatic cancer, he was told that it was incurable and that he would not live long (P18).

Some evidence is better quoted than paraphrased. If an author has found the quickest way to phrase the idea or the words are especially strong, you might want to **use the author's words.** The third line from paragraph 2 quotes Jobs exactly, incorporating his powerful phrases.

> He describes Death as "the single best invention of Life" and "life's change agent" because it "clears out the old to make way for the new" (P21).

5. REFERENCE YOUR EVIDENCE

Whether you paraphrase or quote the author's words, you must include the exact location where the ideas come from. Direct quotes are written in quotation marks. How writers include the reference can vary depending on the piece and the original text. Here the writer puts the paragraph numbers from the original text in parentheses at the end of the sentence.

MAKING EVIDENCE-BASED CLAIMS
FINAL WRITING TASKS

In this unit, you have been developing your skills as a reader who can make text-based claims and prove them with evidence from the text. You have learned to do the following things:

- Uncover key clues in the details, words, and central ideas found in the text
- Make connections among details, central ideas, and text
- Use the details, connections, and evidence you find in the text to form a claim—a stated conclusion—about something you have discovered
- Organize evidence from the text to support your claim and make your case
- Express and explain your claim in writing
- Improve your writing so that others will clearly understand and appreciate your evidence-based claim—and think about the case you have made for it

Your final two writing assignments will provide you with opportunities to use all of these related skills and to demonstrate your proficiency and growth in Making Evidence-Based Claims.

FINAL ASSIGNMENTS

1. **Developing and Writing an Evidence-Based Claim:** On your own, you will read the final part of text in the unit closely and develop an evidence-based claim. To accomplish this, you will do the following:

   a. Read and annotate a new text (or section of text) on your own and use Guiding Questions and a **Forming EBC Tool** to develop an initial claim about the text.

   b. Compare the notes and initial claim you make with those made by other students—reframe or revise your claim.

   c. Complete an **Organizing EBC Tool** to plan subpoints and evidence you will use to explain and support your claim.

   d. Study the **Writing EBC Handout** to know what a written evidence-based claim needs to do, and what examples might look like.

   e. Draft a one- to two-paragraph written presentation and explanation of your claim, making sure that you do the things listed on the **Writing EBC Handout**:

   ⇒ <u>Establish the context</u> by connecting the claim to the text

   ⇒ <u>State the claim clearly</u> to fully communicate your ideas about the text

   ⇒ <u>Organize supporting</u> evidence found in the text

   ⇒ <u>Paraphrase and quote</u> from the text

   ⇒ <u>Reference the evidence</u> drawn from the text

   f. Work with other students to review and improve your draft—and to be sure it is the best possible representation of your claim and your skills as a reader and writer. Work on improving at least one of these aspects of your claim:

   ⇒ How <u>clear</u> your presentation and explanation of your claim is

   ⇒ How <u>defensible</u> (based on the evidence you present) your claim is

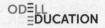

FINAL WRITING TASKS (Continued)

⇒ How well you have <u>presented and referenced evidence</u> to support your claim

⇒ How well you have <u>organized</u> your subpoints and evidence into a unified claim

g. Reflect on how well you have used Literacy Skills in developing this written claim.

2. **Writing and Revising a Global or Comparative Evidence-Based Claim Essay:** On your own, you will plan and draft a multiparagraph essay that presents a global or comparative claim—one based on connections you have found among sections of text you have read in the unit. To accomplish this, you will do the following:

   a. Review the text you have read, the tools you have completed, and the claims you have formed throughout the unit, looking for connections or comparisons.

   b. Use a *Forming EBC Tool* to make a new claim that connects or compares the text you have read or that develops a global conclusion about the meaning of the text.

   c. Use an *Organizing EBC Tool* to plan the subpoints and evidence you will use to explain and support your claim.

   d. Draft a multiparagraph essay that explains, develops, and supports your global or comparative claim—keeping in mind these three criteria for this final writing assignment. Your essay should do the following:

      ⇒ Demonstrate an accurate reading and insightful analysis of the texts you have read in the unit.

      ⇒ Develop a supported claim that is clearly connected to the content of the text.

      ⇒ Successfully accomplish the five key elements of a written evidence-based claim (*Writing EBC Handout*).

   e. Use a collaborative process with other students to review and improve your draft in two key areas: (1) its content (quality of the claim and its evidence) and (2) its organization and expression (unity of the discussion and clarity of the writing).

   f. Reflect on how well you have used Literacy Skills in developing this final explanation.

SKILLS TO BE DEMONSTRATED

As you become a text expert and write your evidence-based claims, think about demonstrating the Literacy Skills you have been working on to the best of your ability. Your teacher will evaluate your work and determine your grade based on how well you are able to do the following things:

Read

- **Attend to Details:** Identify words, details, or quotations that you think are important to understanding the text

- **Interpret Language:** Understand how words are used to express ideas and perspectives

- **Identify Relationships:** Notice important connections among details, ideas, or texts

- **Recognize Perspective:** Identify and explain the author's view of the unit's topic

ODELL
EDUCATION

FINAL WRITING TASKS (Continued)

SKILLS TO BE DEMONSTRATED (Continued)

Think

- **Make Inferences:** Draw sound conclusions from reading and examining the text closely
- **Form a Claim:** State a meaningful conclusion that is well supported by evidence from the text
- **Use Evidence:** Use well-chosen details from the text to support your claim; accurately paraphrase or quote what the author says in the text

Write

- **Present Details:** Insert details and quotations effectively into your essay
- **Organize Ideas:** Organize your claim, supporting ideas, and evidence in a logical order
- **Use Language:** Write clearly so others can understand your claim and supporting ideas
- **Use Conventions:** Correctly use sentence elements, punctuation, and spelling to produce clear writing
- **Publish:** Correctly use, format, and cite textual evidence to support your claim

HABITS TO BE DEVELOPED

Your teacher may also want you to reflect on how well you have used and developed the following habits of text-centered discussion when you worked with others to understand the texts and improve your writing:

- **Engage Actively:** Focus your attention on the assigned tasks when working individually and with others
- **Collaborate:** Work respectfully and productively to help your discussion or review group be successful
- **Communicate Clearly:** Present your ideas and supporting evidence so others can understand them
- **Listen:** Pay attention to ideas from others and take time to think about them
- **Understand Purpose and Process:** Understand why and how a text-centered discussion or peer writing review should be accomplished
- **Revise:** Rethink your ideas and refine your writing based on feedback from others
- **Remaining Open:** Modify and further justify your ideas in response to thinking from others

Note: These skills and habits are also listed on the ***Student Literacy Skills and Academic Habits Checklists***, which you can use to assess your work and the work of other students.

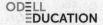

QUESTIONING PATH TOOL

Steve Jobs's Stanford Commencement Address, paragraphs 1–8

APPROACHING: *I determine my reading purposes and take note of key information about the text. I identify the LIPS domain(s) that will guide my initial reading.*

I will initially focus on the author's *perspective* and the *structure* of the speech, then consider *language*, *ideas*, and supporting details. I will think about what the speaker's purpose may be in a commencement speech.

QUESTIONING: *I use Guiding Questions to help me investigate the text (from the **Guiding Questions Handout**).*

1. What do I learn about the author and the purpose for writing the text? [P]

2. What do I notice about how the text is organized or sequenced? [S]

ANALYZING: *I question further to connect and analyze the details I find (from the **Guiding Questions Handout**).*

3. How might I summarize the main ideas of the text and the key supporting details? [I]

DEEPENING: *I consider the questions of others.*

4. At the end of paragraph 4, we learn that Steve Jobs's mother "refused to sign the adoption papers." Why did she do this, and why did she "relent" a few months later?

5. What were the reasons why Steve Jobs "decided to drop out" of college? Why was doing so "one of the best decisions I ever made"?

6. What are the "dots" that Steve Jobs connected between his postcollege experiences and his designing of the first Mac computer?

7. What do you think Steve Jobs means when he says "you can't connect the dots looking forward; you can only connect them looking backwards"? What evidence does he use to support this claim?

EXTENDING: *I pose my own questions.*

ODELL
EDUCATION

APPROACHING TEXTS TOOL

Name _____ Text _____

APPROACHING THE TEXT	
Before reading, I consider what my specific purposes for reading are.	**What are my reading purposes?**
I also take note of key information about the text.	**Title:** **Author:** **Source/Publisher:**
	Text type: **Publication date:**
	What do I already think or understand about the text based on this information?

QUESTIONING THE TEXT	
As I read the text for the first time, I use Guiding Questions that relate to my reading purpose and focus. (*Can be taken from the Guiding Questions Handout.*)	**Guiding Questions for *my first reading* of the text:**
	As I read I mark details on the text that relate to my Guiding Questions.
As I reread, I use questions I have about specific details that have emerged in my reading to focus my analysis and deepen my understanding.	**Text-specific questions to help focus *my rereading* of the text:**

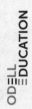
ODELL EDUCATION

ANALYZING DETAILS TOOL

Name _ _ _ _ _ _ _ _ _ _ _ _ _ _ Text _ _ _ _ _ _ _ _ _ _ _ _ _ _ _ _ _ _

Reading purpose:

A question I have about the text:

SEARCHING FOR DETAILS	I read the text closely and mark words and phrases that help me think about my question.		
SELECTING DETAILS I select words or phrases from my search that I think are the most important in thinking about my question.	**Detail 1 (Ref.:**)	**Detail 2 (Ref.:**)	**Detail 3 (Ref.:**)
ANALYZING DETAILS I reread parts of the text and think about the meaning of the details and what they tell me about my question.	**What I think about detail 1:**	**What I think about detail 2:**	**What I think about detail 3:**
CONNECTING DETAILS I compare the details and explain the connections I see among them.	**How I connect the details:**		

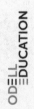

ODELL
EDUCATION

FORMING EVIDENCE-BASED CLAIMS TOOL

Name _____

Text _____

A question I have about the text:

FINDING DETAILS	Detail 1 (Ref.:)	Detail 2 (Ref.:)	Detail 3 (Ref.:)
I find interesting details that are related and that stand out to me from reading the text closely.			

CONNECTING THE DETAILS	What I think about detail 1:	What I think about detail 2:	What I think about detail 3:
I reread and think about the details, and explain the connections I find among them.			

How I connect the details:

MAKING A CLAIM	My claim about the text:
I state a conclusion that I have come to and can support with evidence from the text after reading and thinking about it closely.	

SUPPORTING EVIDENCE-BASED CLAIMS TOOL

Name _ _ _ _ _ _ _ _ _ _ _ _ _ _ _   **Text** _ _ _ _ _ _ _ _ _ _ _ _ _ _ _

CLAIM:

Supporting Evidence	Supporting Evidence

Supporting Evidence

(Reference: _____)   (Reference: _____)   (Reference: _____)

CLAIM:

Supporting Evidence	Supporting Evidence

Supporting Evidence

(Reference: _____)   (Reference: _____)   (Reference: _____)

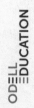

ODELL
EDUCATION

QUESTIONING PATH TOOL

Steve Jobs's Stanford Commencement Address, paragraphs 9–14

APPROACHING:
I determine my reading purposes and take note of key information about the text. I identify the LIPS domain(s) that will guide my initial reading.

I will initially focus on the author's *perspective*, then consider *language*, *ideas*, and supporting details.

QUESTIONING: *I use Guiding Questions to help me investigate the text (from the **Guiding Questions Handout**).*

1. What seems to be the author's point of view? [P]

2. What details or words suggest the author's perspective? [P]

ANALYZING: *I question further to connect and analyze the details I find (from the **Guiding Questions Handout**).*

3. What claims do I find in the text? [I]

DEEPENING: *I consider the questions of others.*

4. In paragraph 10 we learn that between ages twenty and thirty, Steve Jobs experienced great success and great failure. What were his successes, and how did his failure occur?

5. Why might Jobs claim that "getting fired from Apple was the best thing that could have ever happened to me"?

6. What might Jobs mean when he makes the claim: "Sometimes life hits you in the head with a brick"?

7. He then tells his audience two things not to do, beginning his sentences with the word "Don't." How does paragraph 14 further develop the message Jobs is presenting to the graduates?

EXTENDING: *I pose my own questions.*

SUPPORTING EVIDENCE-BASED CLAIMS TOOL

Name _ _ _ _ _ _ _ _ _ _ _ _ _ _ _ _ _ **Text** _ _ _ _ _ _ _ _ _ _ _ _ _ _ _ _ _

CLAIM:

Supporting Evidence	Supporting Evidence	Supporting Evidence
(Reference:)	(Reference:)	(Reference:)

CLAIM:

Supporting Evidence	Supporting Evidence	Supporting Evidence
(Reference:)	(Reference:)	(Reference:)

SUPPORTING EVIDENCE-BASED CLAIMS TOOL

Name _____   Text _____

CLAIM:

Supporting Evidence	Supporting Evidence

(Reference:)   (Reference:)

CLAIM:

Supporting Evidence	Supporting Evidence

(Reference:)   (Reference:)

FORMING EVIDENCE-BASED CLAIMS TOOL

Name _ _ _ _ _ _ _ _ _ _ _ _ _ _ _ Text _ _ _ _ _ _ _ _ _ _ _ _ _ _ _

A question I have about the text:

FINDING DETAILS	Detail 1 (Ref.:)	Detail 2 (Ref.:)	Detail 3 (Ref.:)
I find interesting details that are related and that stand out to me from reading the text closely.			

CONNECTING THE DETAILS	What I think about detail 1:	What I think about detail 2:	What I think about detail 3:
I reread and think about the details, and explain the connections I find among them.			

How I connect the details:

MAKING A CLAIM	My claim about the text:
I state a conclusion that I have come to and can support with evidence from the text after reading and thinking about it closely.	

ODELL EDUCATION

QUESTIONING PATH TOOL

Steve Jobs's Stanford Commencement Address, paragraphs 15–21

APPROACHING:
I determine my reading purposes and take note of key information about the text. I identify the LIPS domain(s) that will guide my initial reading.

I will initially focus on the narrative details of the third story, then the *ideas* the author presents through those details, and finally how he conveys his *perspective* through *language*.

QUESTIONING: *I use Guiding Questions to help me investigate the text (from the **Guiding Questions Handout**).*

1. What do I think the text is mainly about—what is discussed in detail? [I]

2. What claims do I find in the text? [I]

ANALYZING: *I question further to connect and analyze the details I find (from the **Guiding Questions Handout**).*

3. What details or words suggest the author's perspective? [P, L]

4. How does the author's perspective influence his presentation of ideas, themes, or claims? [P]

DEEPENING: *I consider the questions of others.*

5. In paragraphs 18 and 19, we learn important details about Jobs's life and health. What is the sequence of life-changing events that he tells his audience about in his third story, the one "about death"?

6. In paragraph 16, what question does Steve Jobs claim he has asked himself "every morning" "for the past 33 years"? How might Jobs's diagnosis have changed his perspective and the way he thinks about this question?

7. What does Jobs mean when he refers to death as "a useful but purely intellectual concept" in paragraph 20? How might the events of Jobs's life change his previous perspective on death as an "intellectual concept"?

8. At the start of paragraph 17, Jobs makes a claim: "Remembering that I'll be dead soon is the most important tool I've ever encountered to help me make the big choices in life." How does he explain and support this claim?

9. How does Steve Jobs explain the puzzling claim he makes in paragraph 21 that "Death is very likely the single best invention of Life"?

EXTENDING: *I pose my own questions.*

FORMING EVIDENCE-BASED CLAIMS TOOL

Name _ _ _ _ _ _ _ _ _ _ _ Text _

A question I have about the text:

FINDING DETAILS	Detail 1 (Ref.:)	Detail 2 (Ref.:)	Detail 3 (Ref.:)
I find interesting details that are <u>related</u> and that stand out to me from reading the text closely.			

CONNECTING THE DETAILS	What I think about detail 1:	What I think about detail 2:	What I think about detail 3:
I reread and think about the details, and <u>explain</u> the connections I find among them.			

How I connect the details:

MAKING A CLAIM	My claim about the text:
I state a conclusion that I have come to and can support with <u>evidence</u> from the text after reading and thinking about it closely.	

ODELL
EDUCATION

ORGANIZING EVIDENCE-BASED CLAIMS TOOL (2 POINTS)

Name _ Text _ _ _ _ _ _ _ _ _ _ _ _ _ _ _ _ _ _ _

CLAIM:

Point 1

A   Supporting Evidence

(Reference:)

B   Supporting Evidence

(Reference:)

C   Supporting Evidence

(Reference:)

D   Supporting Evidence

(Reference:)

Point 2

A   Supporting Evidence

(Reference:)

B   Supporting Evidence

(Reference:)

C   Supporting Evidence

(Reference:)

D   Supporting Evidence

(Reference:)

ODELL EDUCATION

ORGANIZING EVIDENCE-BASED CLAIMS TOOL (3 POINTS)

Name _ _ _ _ _ _ _ _ _ _ _ _ Text _ _ _ _ _ _ _ _

CLAIM:

Point 1

A	Supporting Evidence

(Reference:)

B	Supporting Evidence

(Reference:)

C	Supporting Evidence

(Reference:)

Point 2

A	Supporting Evidence

(Reference:)

B	Supporting Evidence

(Reference:)

C	Supporting Evidence

(Reference:)

Point 3

A	Supporting Evidence

(Reference:)

B	Supporting Evidence

(Reference:)

C	Supporting Evidence

(Reference:)

ODELL EDUCATION

FORMING EVIDENCE-BASED CLAIMS TOOL

Name _ Text _

A question I have about the text:

FINDING DETAILS	Detail 1 (Ref.:)	Detail 2 (Ref.:)	Detail 3 (Ref.:)
I find interesting details that are related and that stand out to me from reading the text closely.			

CONNECTING THE DETAILS	What I think about detail 1:	What I think about detail 2:	What I think about detail 3:
I reread and think about the details, and explain the connections I find among them.			

How I connect the details:

MAKING A CLAIM	My claim about the text:
I state a conclusion that I have come to and can support with evidence from the text after reading and thinking about it closely.	

ORGANIZING EVIDENCE-BASED CLAIMS TOOL (2 POINTS)

Name _____   Text _____

CLAIM:

Point 1

A Supporting Evidence	B Supporting Evidence
(Reference:)	(Reference:)
C Supporting Evidence	D Supporting Evidence
(Reference:)	(Reference:)

Point 2

A Supporting Evidence	B Supporting Evidence
(Reference:)	(Reference:)
C Supporting Evidence	D Supporting Evidence
(Reference:)	(Reference:)

ORGANIZING EVIDENCE-BASED CLAIMS TOOL (3 POINTS)

Name _ _ _ _ _ _ _ _ _ _ _ _ _ Text _

CLAIM:

Point 1

Point 2

Point 3

A	Supporting Evidence	A	Supporting Evidence	A	Supporting Evidence
(Reference:)		(Reference:)		(Reference:)	
B	Supporting Evidence	B	Supporting Evidence	B	Supporting Evidence
(Reference:)		(Reference:)		(Reference:)	
C	Supporting Evidence	C	Supporting Evidence	C	Supporting Evidence
(Reference:)		(Reference:)		(Reference:)	

ODELL EDUCATION

FORMING EVIDENCE-BASED CLAIMS TOOL

Name _ **Text** _

A question I have about the text:

FINDING DETAILS	**Detail 1 (Ref.:**)	**Detail 2 (Ref.:**)	**Detail 3 (Ref.:**)
I find interesting details that are <u>related</u> and that stand out to me from reading the text closely.			

CONNECTING THE DETAILS	**What I think about detail 1:**	**What I think about detail 2:**	**What I think about detail 3:**
I reread and think about the details, and <u>explain</u> the connections I find among them.			

How I connect the details:

MAKING A CLAIM	**My claim about the text:**
I state a conclusion that I have come to and can support with <u>evidence</u> from the text after reading and thinking about it closely.	

ODELL EDUCATION

QUESTIONING PATH TOOL

Name: _____ **Text:** _____

APPROACHING: *I determine my reading purposes and take note of key information about the text. I identify the LIPS domain(s) that will guide my initial reading.*

Purpose:

Key information:

LIPS domain(s):

QUESTIONING: *I use Guiding Questions to help me investigate the text (from the **Guiding Questions Handout**).*

1.

2.

ANALYZING: *I question further to connect and analyze the details I find (from the **Guiding Questions Handout**).*

1.

2.

DEEPENING: *I consider the questions of others.*

1.

2.

3.

EXTENDING: *I pose my own questions.*

1.

2.

FORMING EVIDENCE-BASED CLAIMS TOOL

Name _ Text _

A question I have about the text:

FINDING DETAILS	Detail 1 (Ref.:)	Detail 2 (Ref.:)	Detail 3 (Ref.:)
I find interesting details that are <u>related</u> and that stand out to me from reading the text closely.			

CONNECTING THE DETAILS	What I think about detail 1:	What I think about detail 2:	What I think about detail 3:
I reread and think about the details, and <u>explain</u> the connections I find among them.			
	How I connect the details:		

MAKING A CLAIM	My claim about the text:
I state a conclusion that I have come to and can support with <u>evidence</u> from the text after reading and thinking about it closely.	

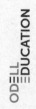

ODELL
EDUCATION

ORGANIZING EVIDENCE-BASED CLAIMS TOOL (2 POINTS)

Name _ _ _ _ _ _ _ _ _ _ _ _ _ _ _ _ Text _

CLAIM:

Point 1

A	Supporting Evidence	B	Supporting Evidence
(Reference:)		(Reference:)	
C	Supporting Evidence	D	Supporting Evidence
(Reference:)		(Reference:)	

Point 2

A	Supporting Evidence	B	Supporting Evidence
(Reference:)		(Reference:)	
C	Supporting Evidence	D	Supporting Evidence
(Reference:)		(Reference:)	

ORGANIZING EVIDENCE-BASED CLAIMS TOOL (3 POINTS)

Name _ _ _ _ _ _ _ _ _ _ _ _ _ Text _ _ _ _ _ _ _ _ _ _ _ _ _

CLAIM:

Point 1	Point 2	Point 3
A Supporting Evidence	**A** Supporting Evidence	**A** Supporting Evidence
(Reference:)	(Reference:)	(Reference:)
B Supporting Evidence	**B** Supporting Evidence	**B** Supporting Evidence
(Reference:)	(Reference:)	(Reference:)
C Supporting Evidence	**C** Supporting Evidence	**C** Supporting Evidence
(Reference:)	(Reference:)	(Reference:)

FORMING EVIDENCE-BASED CLAIMS TOOL

Name _ _ _ _ _ _ _ _ _ _ _ Text _ _ _ _ _ _ _ _ _ _ _ _ _ _ _ _ _

A question I have about the text:

FINDING DETAILS	Detail 1 (Ref.:)	Detail 2 (Ref.:)	Detail 3 (Ref.:)
I find interesting details that are <u>related</u> and that stand out to me from reading the text closely.			

CONNECTING THE DETAILS	What I think about detail 1:	What I think about detail 2:	What I think about detail 3:
I reread and think about the details, and <u>explain</u> the connections I find among them.			

How I connect the details:

MAKING A CLAIM	My claim about the text:
I state a conclusion that I have come to and can support with <u>evidence</u> from the text after reading and thinking about it closely.	

ODELL
EDUCATION

SUPPORTING EVIDENCE-BASED CLAIMS TOOL

Name _ _ _ _ _ _ _ _ _ _ _ _ _ _ _ _ _ _   **Text** _ _ _ _ _ _ _ _ _ _ _ _ _ _ _ _ _ _

CLAIM:

Supporting Evidence	Supporting Evidence
Supporting Evidence	

(Reference:)   (Reference:

CLAIM:

Supporting Evidence	Supporting Evidence
Supporting Evidence	

(Reference:)   (Reference:

ORGANIZING EVIDENCE-BASED CLAIMS TOOL (2 POINTS)

Name _ _ _ _ _ _ _ _ _ _ _ _ _ _ _ _ _ _ _ Text _

CLAIM:

Point 1

A Supporting Evidence	B Supporting Evidence
(Reference:)	(Reference:)
C Supporting Evidence	D Supporting Evidence
(Reference:)	(Reference:)

Point 2

A Supporting Evidence	B Supporting Evidence
(Reference:)	(Reference:)
C Supporting Evidence	D Supporting Evidence
(Reference:)	(Reference:)

ORGANIZING EVIDENCE-BASED CLAIMS TOOL (3 POINTS)

Name _

Text _ _ _ _ _ _ _ _ _ _ _ _ _ _ _ _ _ _ _

CLAIM:

Point 1

Point 2

Point 3

A   Supporting Evidence

(Reference:)

B   Supporting Evidence

(Reference:)

C   Supporting Evidence

(Reference:)

A   Supporting Evidence

(Reference:)

B   Supporting Evidence

(Reference:)

C   Supporting Evidence

(Reference:)

A   Supporting Evidence

(Reference:)

B   Supporting Evidence

(Reference:)

C   Supporting Evidence

(Reference:)

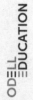

ODELL EDUCATION

PART 3: STUDENT ACADEMIC HABITS CHECKLIST

HABITS DEVELOPED	DESCRIPTORS	EVIDENCE OF USING THE HABIT	THINGS TO IMPROVE ON
COLLABORATING	Pays attention to and respects other participants Works productively with others to complete the task and enrich the discussion		
COMMUNICATING CLEARLY	Uses clear language to communicate ideas and claims Uses relevant details to explain and support thinking		
LISTENING	Pays attention to new information and ideas from others Considers others' ideas thoughtfully		

PART 4: STUDENT ACADEMIC HABITS CHECKLIST

HABITS DEVELOPED	DESCRIPTORS	EVIDENCE OF USING THE HABIT	THINGS TO IMPROVE ON
UNDERSTANDING PURPOSE AND PROCESS	Understands and uses the collaborative writing workshop process Uses literacy skills criteria to frame questions, responses, and feedback		
LISTENING	Pays attention to new information and ideas from others Considers others' ideas thoughtfully		
REMAINING OPEN	Avoids explanations or justifications for what they as writers have tried to do Frames text-based questions to probe their readers' observations		
REVISING	Uses criteria to rethink, refine, or revise work Uses observations from peers to inform improvement		

ODELL
EDUCATION

STUDENT MAKING EVIDENCE-BASED CLAIMS LITERACY SKILLS CHECKLIST

	LITERACY SKILLS USED IN THIS UNIT	✔	EVIDENCE Demonstrating the SKILLS
READING	1. **Attending to Details:** Identifies words, details, or quotations that are important to understanding the text		
	2. **Interpreting Language:** Understands how words are used to express ideas and perspectives		
	3. **Identifying Relationships:** Notices important connections among details, ideas, or texts		
	4. **Recognizing Perspective:** Identifies and explains the author's view of the text's topic		
THINKING	5. **Making Inferences:** Draws sound conclusions from reading and examining the text closely		
	6. **Forming Claims:** States a meaningful conclusion that is well-supported by evidence from the text		
	7. **Using Evidence:** Uses well-chosen details from the text to explain and support claims; accurately paraphrases or quotes		
WRITING	8. **Presenting Details:** Inserts details and quotations effectively into written or spoken explanations		
	9. **Organizing Ideas:** Organizes claims, supporting ideas, and evidence in a logical order		
	10. **Using Language:** Writes and speaks clearly so others can understand claims and ideas		
	11. **Using Conventions:** Correctly uses sentence elements, punctuation, and spelling to produce clear writing		
	12. **Publishing:** Correctly uses, formats, and cites textual evidence to support claims		
General comments:			

ODELL EDUCATION

STUDENT MAKING EVIDENCE-BASED CLAIMS ACADEMIC HABITS CHECKLIST

Academic Habits Used in This Unit	✔	EVIDENCE Demonstrating the HABITS
1. **Engaging Actively:** Focuses attention on the task when working individually and with others		
2. **Collaborating:** Works respectfully and productively to help a group be successful		
3. **Communicating Clearly:** Presents ideas and supporting evidence so others can understand them		
4. **Listening:** Pays attention to ideas from others and takes time to think about them		
5. **Understanding Purpose and Process:** Understands why and how a task should be accomplished		
6. **Revising:** Rethinks ideas and refines work based on feedback from others		
7. **Remaining Open:** Modifies and further justifies ideas in response to thinking from others		
General comments:		

UNIT 3

RESEARCHING TO DEEPEN UNDERSTANDING

DEVELOPING CORE LITERACY PROFICIENCIES

GRADE 6

Prehistoric Cave Art

GOAL

In this unit you will develop your proficiency as an investigator and user of information. You will learn how to do the following:

1. Have an inquiring mind and ask good questions.
2. Search for information—in texts, interviews, and on the Internet—that can help you answer your questions.
3. Record and organize the information you find.
4. Decide what is relevant and trustworthy in the sources of your information.
5. Come to a Research-Based Perspective on a topic.
6. Clearly communicate what you have learned and "tell the story" of how you've come to learn it.

TOPIC

In this unit, you will explore the unbelievable pictures that prehistoric humans painted in caves. Through videos, images, and texts, you will learn about the art as well as the people who created cave paintings. As the unit progresses, you will identify aspects of the topic you would like to learn more about.

ACTIVITIES

Throughout the unit, you will watch videos, read texts, and discuss the cave art with your class. As a class you will determine what you want to explore through research. As you read sources closely, you will keep an organized portfolio. Using your notes, you will express your new knowledge in a reflective research narrative.

TERMS AND DEFINITIONS USED IN THIS UNIT

Topic:

the general topic chosen for class exploration

Area of Investigation:

a specific question, problem, or subtopic about the general topic that you research

Inquiry Questions:

questions you ask and try to answer about your Areas of Investigation

Research Portfolio:

the binder or electronic folder where you store and organize all your personal research materials

Research Plan:

an organizer that shows you the research process you follow

RESEARCHING TO DEEPEN UNDERSTANDING LITERACY TOOLBOX

In *Researching to Deepen Understanding*, you will begin to build your "literacy toolbox" by learning how to use the following handouts, tools and checklists organized in your Student Edition.

 **TOOLS**

In *Researching to Deepen Understanding*, you will further develop and apply your literacy toolbox by learning how to use the following tools organized in your Student Edition. You may also apply tools from other Developing Core Literacy Proficiencies units:

Forming Evidence-Based Claims Research Tool

from the *Making Evidence-Based Claims* unit (with Inquiry Question)

Organizing Evidence-Based Claims Research Tool

from the *Making Evidence-Based Claims* unit (with Inquiry Question)

Taking Notes Tool

This tool helps you make and organize notes from the various sources you find throughout your research.

Exploring a Topic Tool

This tool helps you think about potential areas of the topic you want to explore through research.

Potential Sources Tool

This tool helps you collect and organize information on sources you find that might be useful in your research.

Research Evaluation Tool

This tool helps you work with your peers and teacher to determine if you have found enough information on your Area of Investigation.

HANDOUTS

To support your work with the texts and the tools, you will be able to use the following informational handouts:

Research Plan

This handout presents the process you will follow during the various stages of inquiry.

Research Portfolio

This handout will help you to organize your tools and analysis throughout the research process.

Attending to Details Handout

from the *Reading Closely* unit

Guiding Questions Handout

from the *Reading Closely* unit

Posing Inquiry Questions Handout

This handout helps you come up with good questions to ask about a topic. These questions help you find out important information throughout your research.

Assessing Sources Handout

This handout helps you evaluate how useful a potential source will be for your research.

Connecting Ideas Handout

This handout gives you examples of words to use in making connections among ideas in your writing.

Researching to Deepen Understanding Final Writing Task Handout

This handout explains to you what you will be doing in the final assignment for this unit: writing a reflective research narrative that tells the story of how you arrived at your Research-Based Perspective on the topic and communicates your experience with the inquiry process. The handout will also help you know what your teacher will be looking for so you can be successful writing your narrative.

CHECKLISTS

You will also use these checklists throughout the unit to support peer- and self-review:

Researching to Deepen Understanding Skills and Habits Checklist

This checklist presents and briefly describes the Literacy Skills and Habits you will be working on during the unit. You can use it to remind you of what you are trying to learn. You can also use it to

Developing Core Literacy Proficiencies

reflect on what you have done when reading, discussing, or writing. It can help you give feedback to other students about their research. Your teacher may use it to let you know about your areas of strength and areas in which you need to improve.

Area Evaluation and Research Evaluation Checklists

These checklists help you keep track of the different activities you need to do while researching the topic. They also can help you think about how clearly you are able to express your topic and questions.

RESEARCHING TO DEEPEN UNDERSTANDING COMMON TEXTS

Prehistoric Cave Art

NOTE
The unit uses texts that are accessible for free on the Internet without any login information, membership requirements, or purchase. Because of the ever-changing nature of website addresses, specific links are not provided. Teachers and students can locate these texts through web searches using the information provided.

AUTHOR	DATE
Text 1: *The Chauvet-Pont-d'Arc Cave*	
French Ministry of Culture and Communication (with English translation)	NA
Text 2: "Forgotten Cave in France Was Hiding Stone Age Art"	
Newsela.com	April 15, 2015
Text 3: "Ancient Humans' Art Is Older Than We Thought"	
Newsela.com	October 14, 2014
Text 4.1: *The Lascaux Cave Virtual Tour*	
French Ministry of Culture and Communication (available in English by clicking on "Accessibilité")	NA
Text 4.2: "Lascaux Cave Paintings—An Introduction"	
Bradshaw Foundation	2011
Text 5: *The Chauvet-Pont-d'Arc Cave*	
French Ministry of Culture and Communication (with English translation)	NA
Text 6.1: "Cave and Rock Art"	
The Blackbirch Encyclopedia of Science & Invention	2001
Text 6.2: "Hands across Time"	
Mary Reina	2008

Text 7: "Why Did Prehistoric People Make Cave Art?"	
Adam Benton	July 23, 2013
Text 8: "Cave Art Found: Was It a Prehistoric Preschool?"	
Deepa Gopal	October 10, 2011
Text 9: "Origins of Religion"	
Frank E. Smitha	2009–2013
Text 10: "Ancient Cave Behavior"	
Emily Sohn	October 24, 2007
Text 11: "Neanderthals: The Oldest Cave Painters"	
Interview by Ira Flatow	June 15, 2012
Text 12: "Stone Age Jottings"	
New Scientists	February 20, 2010

RESEARCHING TO
DEEPEN UNDERSTANDING

DEVELOPING CORE LITERACY
PROFICIENCIES

GRADE 6

Literacy Toolbox

ODELL
EDUCATION

STUDENT RESEARCH PLAN

STUDENT RESEARCH PLAN—GRADE 6		TOOLS AND HANDOUTS
I. INITIATING INQUIRY *I determine what I want to know about a topic and develop Inquiry Questions that I will investigate.*	**1. Introducing the Unit**	Student Research Plan Questioning Path Tool Exploring a Topic Tool Potential Sources Tool Area Evaluation Checklist Posing Inquiry Questions Handout
	2. Exploring a Topic	
	3. Recording Research Interests and Potential Sources	
	4. Exploring a Topic Further	
	5. Choosing an Area of Investigation	
	6. Generating Inquiry Questions	
II. GATHERING INFORMATION *I take notes on sources that will help me answer my Inquiry Questions and define the scope of my investigation.*	**1. Introduction to Sources**	Potential Sources Tool Assessing Sources Handout Taking Notes Tool
	2. Assessing Sources	
	3. Making and Recording Notes	
III. DEEPENING UNDERSTANDING *I analyze sources to deepen my understanding and answer my Inquiry Questions.*	**1. Reading Sources Closely**	Assessing Sources Handout Forming Evidence-Based Claims Tool Attending to Details Handout Connecting Ideas Handout Writing Evidence-Based Claims Handout
	2. Writing Evidence-Based Claims About Sources	
	3. Discussing Understanding of the Area of Investigation	
IV. FINALIZING INQUIRY *I synthesize my information to determine what I have learned and what more I need to know about my Area of Investigation. I gather and analyze more information to complete my inquiry.*	**1. Addressing an Inquiry Question**	Forming Evidence-Based Claims Tool Organizing Evidence-Based Claims Tool Connecting Ideas Handout Research Checklist
	2. Organizing Evidence	
	3. Evaluating Research	
	4. Refining Inquiry	
V. DEVELOPING AND COMMUNICATING AN EVIDENCE-BASED PERSPECTIVE *I review and synthesize my research to develop and communicate an evidence-based perspective on my Area of Investigation.*	**1. Reviewing Research Portfolios**	Potential Sources Tools Organizing Evidence-Based Claims Tool Connecting Ideas Handout Writing Evidence-Based Claims Handout Connecting Ideas Handout
	2. Expressing An Evidence-Based Perspective	
	3. Writing A Bibliography	
	4. Communicating A Final Evidence-Based Product	

RESEARCH PORTFOLIO DESCRIPTION

The Research Portfolio helps you store and organize your findings and analysis throughout every step of the research process. Various tools help you develop a research strategy and record, analyze, and annotate your sources. Every time you complete a tool or annotate a source, file it in the corresponding section of your portfolio. Keeping an organized portfolio helps you make connections, see what you already have, and determine what you still have left to investigate. It will also provide everything you need to write your conclusions when you finish your research. The portfolio may be in either electronic or paper format.

PORTFOLIO SECTIONS	CONTENT
SECTION 1: DEFINING AN AREA OF INVESTIGATION *This section stores all the work you do exploring the Topic and choosing an Area of Investigation.*	Exploring a Topic Area Evaluation Checklist Potential Sources
SECTION 2: GATHERING AND ANALYZING INFORMATION *This section stores all the information you gather throughout your investigation. It also stores your notes and analysis of sources.* *All the tools should be grouped by source.*	Potential Sources Annotated Sources Personal Drafts Taking Notes Forming EBC
SECTION 3: DRAWING CONCLUSIONS *This section stores your Notes and EBCs about Inquiry Questions, your research evaluation, and the personal perspective that you come to at the end of your inquiry.* *Group the Taking Notes, Forming EBC or Organizing EBC by Inquiry Question.*	Taking Notes Forming EBC Organizing EBC Evidence-Based Perspective

ODELL
EDUCATION

ASSESSING SOURCES

ASSESSING A SOURCE'S ACCESSIBILITY AND INTEREST LEVEL

Consider your initial experience in reading the text, how well you understand it, and whether it seems interesting to you:

ACCESSIBILITY TO YOU AS A READER	INTEREST AND MEANING FOR YOU AS A READER
• Am I able to read and comprehend the text easily? • How do the text's structure and formatting either help or hinder me in reading it? • Do I have adequate background knowledge to understand the terminology, information, and ideas in the text?	• Does the text present ideas or information that I find interesting? • Which of my Inquiry Paths will the text provide information for? • Which inquiry questions does the text help me answer? How?

ASSESSING A SOURCE'S CREDIBILITY

Look at the information you can find about the text in the following areas, and consider the following questions to assess a source text's credibility:

PUBLISHER	DATE	AUTHOR	TYPE
• What is the publisher's relationship to the topic area? • What economic stake might the publisher have in the topic area? • What political stake might the publisher have in the topic area?	• When was the text first published? • How current is the information on the topic? • How does the publishing date relate to the history of the topic?	• What are the author's qualifications or credentials relative to the topic area? • What is the author's personal relationship to the topic area? • What economic or political stakes might the author have in the topic area?	• What type of text is it: explanation, informational article, feature, research study, op-ed, essay, argument, other? • What is the purpose of the text with respect to the topic area?

ASSESSING A SOURCE'S RELEVANCE AND RICHNESS

Using your Area of Investigation as a reference, consider the following questions:

RELEVANCE TO TOPIC AND PURPOSE	RELEVANCE TO AREA OF INVESTIGATION	SCOPE AND RICHNESS
• What information does the text provide on the topic? • How might the text help me accomplish the purpose for my research? • Does the text provide accurate information?	• How is the text related to the specific area I am investigating? • Which of my paths of inquiry might the text provide information for? • Which inquiry questions might the text help me address? How?	• How long is the text and what is the scope of the topic areas it addresses? • How extensive and supported is the information it provides? • How does the information in the text relate to other texts?

POSING INQUIRY QUESTIONS

Successful research results from posing good Inquiry Questions. When you have to solve a difficult problem or want to investigate a complex idea or issue, **developing questions about things you need to know helps guide your research and analysis**. But not all questions are created equal. Some lead to dead ends, and others open up vistas of knowledge and understanding ... or best of all: *more questions!*

GENERATING QUESTIONS

Generating questions is most fun and effective with friends—the more minds the merrier. And **starting with lots of questions** helps you find the best ones. When brainstorming questions, consider many things about your Area of Investigation, for instance:

- **How is it defined?**
- **Where did it originate?**
- **What is its history?**
- **What are its important places, things, people, and experts?**
- **What are its major aspects?**
- **What are its causes and implications?**
- **What other things is it connected to or associated with?**

SELECTING AND REFINING QUESTIONS

Once you have a huge list of possible questions, select and refine them by asking yourself a few things about them:

Are you genuinely interested in answering your question?

Research requires hard work and endurance. If you don't care about your questions you won't do the work to answer them. The best questions are about things you actually want and need to know.

Can your question truly be answered through your research?

Some questions are unanswerable (How many walnuts are there in the world?) or take years to answer (What is the meaning of life?). Your Inquiry Questions must put you on a reachable path.

Is your question clear?

Can you pose your question in a way that you and others understand what you are asking? If it's confusing, then perhaps you are asking more than one thing. That's great: just break it into two questions. The more good Inquiry Questions you have the better.

What sort of answers does your question require?

Interesting, meaningful research comes from interesting questions. Good inquiry questions are rich enough to support lots of investigation that may even lead to multiple answers and more questions. Questions that can be answered with a simple yes or no generally do not make good Inquiry Questions.

Do you already know what the answer is?

Good Inquiry Questions are actually questions. If you already have answered the questions for yourself, then you won't really be inquiring through your research. If you already know what you think, then you won't get the true reward of research: a deeper knowledge and understanding of things you want to know about.

ODELL
EDUCATION

CONNECTING IDEAS

USING TRANSITIONAL WORDS AND PHRASES

Transitional words and phrases create links between your ideas when you are speaking and writing. They help your audience understand the logic of your thoughts. When using transitional words, make sure that they are the right match for what you want to express. And remember, transition words work best when they are connecting two or more strong ideas that are clearly stated. Here is a list of transitional words and phrases that you can use for different purposes.

GIVE AN EXAMPLE OR ILLUSTRATE AN IDEA
- to illustrate
- to demonstrate
- specifically
- for instance
- as an illustration
- for example

MAKE SURE YOUR THINKING IS CLEARLY UNDERSTOOD
- that is to say
- in other words
- to explain
- i.e., (that is)
- to clarify
- to rephrase it
- to put it another way

COMPARE IDEAS OR SHOW HOW IDEAS ARE SIMILAR
- in the same way
- by the same token
- similarly
- in like manner
- likewise
- in similar fashion

CONTRAST IDEAS OR SHOW HOW THEY ARE DIFFERENT
- nevertheless
- but
- however
- otherwise
- on the contrary
- in contrast
- on the other hand

ADD RELATED INFORMATION
- furthermore
- moreover
- too
- also
- again
- in addition
- next
- further
- finally
- and, or, nor

EXPLAIN HOW ONE THING CAUSES ANOTHER
- because
- since
- on account of
- for that reason

EXPLAIN THE EFFECT OR RESULT OF SOMETHING
- therefore
- consequently
- accordingly
- thus
- hence
- as a result

EXPLAIN YOUR PURPOSE
- in order that
- so that
- to that end, to this end
- for this purpose
- for this reason

LIST RELATED INFORMATION
- First, second, third…
- First, then, also, finally

QUALIFY SOMETHING
- almost
- nearly
- probably
- never
- always
- frequently
- perhaps
- maybe
- although

RESEARCHING TO DEEPEN UNDERSTANDING FINAL WRITING TASK

In this unit, you have been developing your skills as a researcher by doing the following:

- Exploring a topic with your learning community
- Posing Inquiry Questions
- Assessing and analyzing sources
- Making claims about sources
- Maintaining an organized Research Portfolio
- Developing an Evidence-Based Perspective on the topic

Now you will have an opportunity to share what you've learned in a short reflective research narrative. Your narrative should clearly express your understanding on the topic and tell the story of how you have developed your new knowledge. *It does not need to fully summarize and include all of your research.*

REFLECTIVE RESEARCH NARRATIVE

In the reflective research narrative you will do the following:

- Tell a story about what you've learned about the topic through your investigation
- Use notes and claims from your portfolio you have already written
- Clearly connect your ideas to the sources where you have found them
- Reflect on what you have learned about the research process

To write this narrative, you will do the following:

1. Review your Research Portfolio.
   a. Review the materials you have compiled and organized in your Research Portfolio:
   ⇒ *Taking Notes Tools*
   ⇒ *Forming EBC Research Tools*
   ⇒ *Organizing EBC Research Tools*
   ⇒ *Written Evidence-Based Claim(s)*
2. Think about your perspective by considering and discussing any number of the following questions:
   a. Before starting my inquiry, what did I think about the topic? How did I view or understand it?
   b. What specific steps did I take to research the topic? How did I address and answer my Inquiry Questions?
   c. Which sources were the most interesting to me and why? What specifically did I find interesting about the sources?
   d. What did I learn and discover about my Area of Investigation and Inquiry Question(s)?
   e. What Inquiry Questions did I research but did not lead me anywhere?

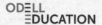

FINAL WRITING TASK (Continued)

  f. What did I learn from my peers about the topic?

  g. What moments were key in developing my understanding of the topic? When did I get something major about the topic?

  h. What do I now think about the topic I have investigated, based on the research and reading I have done? What is my own perspective?

  i. What did I learn about the research process? Where did I struggle and where did I triumph?

3. Think of several different ways you have come to understand cave art based on the texts you have read.

  a. Select one or two of these ideas that match your own understanding, and return to the question:

  ⇒ What do I think about this aspect of cave art?

  b. Your response can be used as an Evidence-Based Perspective that you can work into your narrative.

4. Develop an outline of your reflective research narrative.

  a. Use your *Forming EBC Tools*, *Written EBC*, and *Organizing EBC Tools* to develop an outline of your narrative.

5. Using the *Writing EBC* and the *Connecting Ideas Handouts* as guides, write a first draft your Evidence-Based Perspective paper.

  a. Explain and support your perspective by presenting a set of connected claims based on your *Forming EBC Tools*, *Written EBC*, and *Organizing EBC Tools* (you can use the *Writing EBC Handout* for help).

  b. Use your *Taking Notes Tools* to include evidence from relevant texts to support your claims, accurately quoting and paraphrasing. (Depending on your perspective, you may not use all of them to write your paper.)

  c. Order your sentences and paragraphs to clearly explain your research story and perspective (you can use the *Connecting Ideas Handouts*.)

  d. Use appropriate tone and connecting words and phrases.

6. Review a model reflective research narrative.

  a. Use Guiding Questions to make text-based comments about the model paper.

7. Finalize your reflective research narrative based on what you have learned from the model narrative.

  a. Refine your own perspective and evidence based on what you have learned and discussed while reviewing the model paper.

  b. Check to see if your perspective is clearly stated. You may need to go back to your *Forming EBC Tools* and *Organizing EBC Tools* to help clarify your perspective.

  c. Check to see if you have enough evidence to support your perspective. You may need to go back to your *Organizing EBC Tools* and *Taking Notes Tools* to see if you need to include more details.

  d. Order your sentences and paragraphs to clearly explain your perspective (you can use the *Connecting Ideas Handouts*).

  e. Use a chronological format to recount the steps you took from beginning to end of the research process.

FINAL WRITING TASK (Continued)

REFLECTIVE RESEARCH NARRATIVE (Continued)

    f. Include a reflection on your experience with the inquiry process.

    g. Use appropriate tone and connecting words and phrases.

8. Self- and Peer-Review of your reflective research narrative

    a. Use the following Guiding Review Questions and criteria to both self- and peer-review your reflective research narrative:

    ⇒ Do I reflect on how I originally thought of the topic before I started to research it?

    ⇒ Do I recount the specific steps I took to think of Inquiry Questions about the Area of Investigation?

    ⇒ Do I tell how I read and analyzed texts to help answer my Inquiry Questions?

    ⇒ Do I clearly communicate how I arrived at my Research-Based Perspective?

    ⇒ What is the perspective and is it clearly stated?

    ⇒ Is the claim well supported, and is there enough to explain or defend my perspective?

    ⇒ Does the evidence from the sources sufficiently support the perspective and claims?

    ⇒ Are the sources cited accurately and consistently?

    ⇒ What can be added or revised to better express the perspective?

9. Complete any additional drafts and peer reviews of your paper as instructed.

SKILLS AND HABITS TO BE DEMONSTRATED

As you develop a fine-tuned perspective on the topic, think about demonstrating the Literacy Skills and Academic Habits listed in the following to the best of your ability. Your teacher will evaluate your work and determine your grade based on how well you do the following:

Identify Relationships: Notice important connections among details, ideas, and texts

Make Inferences: Draw sound conclusions from examining a text closely

Summarize: Correctly explains what a text says about a topic

Question: Develop questions and lines of inquiry that lead to important ideas

Recognize Perspective: Identifie and explains the author's view of the text's topic

Evaluate Information: Assess the relevance and credibility of information in texts

Form Claims: State a meaningful conclusion that is well supported by evidence from texts

Use Evidence: Use well-chosen details from texts to explain and support claims; accurately paraphrases or quotes

Organize Ideas: Organize claims, supporting ideas, and evidence in a logical order

Publish: Use effective formatting and citations when paraphrasing, quoting, and listing sources

Reflect Critically: Use literacy concepts to discuss and evaluate personal and peer learning

Generate Ideas: Generate and develops ideas, positions, products, and solutions to problems

ODELL
EDUCATION

FINAL WRITING TASK (Continued)

SKILLS AND HABITS TO BE DEMONSTRATED (Continued)
Organize Work: Maintain materials so that they can be used effectively and efficiently **Complete Tasks:** Finish short and extended tasks by established deadlines **Understand Purpose and Process:** Understand why and how a task should be accomplished *Note*: These skills and habits are also listed on the ***Student Literacy Skills and Academic Habits Checklist*** in your **Literacy Toolbox,** which you can use to assess your work and the work of other students.

EXPLORING A TOPIC TOOL

Name _ _ _ _ _ _ _ _ _ _ _ _ _ **Topic** _ _ _ _ _ _ _ _ _

Write a brief account of the class conversation about the topic describing what you know at this point about some of its aspects:

POTENTIAL AREA OF INVESTIGATION 1
In a few words, describe an area within the topic that you would like to know more about:
Explain why you are interested in this area of the topic:
Express your potential Area of Investigation as a question or problem:

ODELL
EDUCATION

EXPLORING A TOPIC TOOL (Continued)

Name _ _ _ _ _ _ _ _ _ _ _   Topic _

POTENTIAL AREA OF INVESTIGATION 2	POTENTIAL AREA OF INVESTIGATION 3	POTENTIAL AREA OF INVESTIGATION 4
In a few words, describe what you would like to know more about within the topic:	In a few words, describe what you would like to know more about within the topic:	In a few words, describe what you would like to know more about within the topic:
Explain why you are interested in this:	Explain why you are interested in this:	Explain why you are interested in this:
Express your potential area of investigation as a question or problem:	Express your potential area of investigation as a question or problem:	Express your potential area of investigation as a question or problem:

QUESTIONING PATH TOOL

Name: _____ **Text:** _____

APPROACHING: *I determine my reading purposes and take note of key information about the text. I identify the LIPS domain(s) that will guide my initial reading.*	Purpose: Key information: LIPS domain(s):
QUESTIONING: *I use Guiding Questions to help me investigate the text (from the **Guiding Questions Handout**).*	1. 2.
ANALYZING: *I question further to connect and analyze the details I find (from the **Guiding Questions Handout**).*	1. 2.
DEEPENING: *I consider the questions of others.*	1. 2. 3.
EXTENDING: *I pose my own questions.*	1. 2.

ODELL EDUCATION

POTENTIAL SOURCES TOOL

Name _ _ _ _ _ _ _ _ _ _ **Topic** _ _ _ _ _ _ _ _ _ _ _ _ _ _ _

Area of Investigation _

SOURCE

No.	Title:
	Author:

Location:

Publication date:

Text type:

Connection to Inquiry Quest::

General Content/Key Ideas/Personal Comments:

Credibility: [ ] High [ ] Medium [ ] Low

Relevance/Richness: [ ] High [ ] Medium [ ] Low

Accessibility/Interest: [ ] High [ ] Medium [ ] Low

SOURCE

No.	Title:
	Author:

Location:

Publication date:

Text type:

Connection to Inquiry Quest::

General Content/Key Ideas/Personal Comments:

Credibility: [ ] High [ ] Medium [ ] Low

Relevance/Richness: [ ] High [ ] Medium [ ] Low

Accessibility/Interest: [ ] High [ ] Medium [ ] Low

SOURCE

No.	Title:
	Author:

Location:

Publication date:

Text type:

Connection to Inquiry Quest::

General Content/Key Ideas/Personal Comments:

Credibility: [ ] High [ ] Medium [ ] Low

Relevance/Richness: [ ] High [ ] Medium [ ] Low

Accessibility/Interest: [ ] High [ ] Medium [ ] Low

POTENTIAL SOURCES TOOL

Name _ _ _ _ _ _ _ _ _ _ _ _ _ **Topic** _ _ _ _ _ _ _ _ _ _ _

Area of Investigation _ _ _ _ _ _ _ _ _ _ _ _ _ _ _

SOURCE

Title: _____

Location: _____

No. _____ Author: _____

Text type: _____ Publication date: _____

General Content/Key Ideas/Personal Comments:

Connection to Inquiry Quest.:

Accessibility/Interest: [ ] High [ ] Medium [ ] Low

Credibility: [ ] High [ ] Medium [ ] Low

Relevance/Richness: [ ] High [ ] Medium [ ] Low

SOURCE

Title: _____

Location: _____

No. _____ Author: _____

Text type: _____ Publication date: _____

General Content/Key Ideas/Personal Comments:

Connection to Inquiry Quest.:

Accessibility/Interest: [ ] High [ ] Medium [ ] Low

Credibility: [ ] High [ ] Medium [ ] Low

Relevance/Richness: [ ] High [ ] Medium [ ] Low

SOURCE

Title: _____

Location: _____

No. _____ Author: _____

Text type: _____ Publication date: _____

General Content/Key Ideas/Personal Comments:

Connection to Inquiry Quest.:

Accessibility/Interest: [ ] High [ ] Medium [ ] Low

Credibility: [ ] High [ ] Medium [ ] Low

Relevance/Richness: [ ] High [ ] Medium [ ] Low

ODELL EDUCATION

TAKING NOTES TOOL

Name _

Source(s) _

Inquiry Question/Path _ _ _ _ _ _ _ _ _ _ _ _ _ _

REFERENCE	DETAILS	COMMENTS
Source no. and location in the source:	I record details, ideas, or information that I find in my sources that help me answer my Inquiry Questions:	I explain the reason why I think they are important and write personal comments:

TAKING NOTES TOOL

Name _

Source(s) _ _ _ _ _ _ _ _ _ _ _ _ _ _ _ _ _ _ _

Inquiry Question/Path _ _ _ _ _ _ _ _ _ _ _ _

REFERENCE	DETAILS	COMMENTS
Source no. and location in the source:	I record details, ideas, or information that I find in my sources that help me answer my Inquiry Questions:	I explain the reason why I think they are important and write personal comments:

ODELL
EDUCATION

TAKING NOTES TOOL

Name _

Source(s) _

Inquiry Question/Path _ _ _ _ _ _ _ _ _ _ _ _

REFERENCE	DETAILS	COMMENTS
Source no. and location in the source:	*I record details, ideas, or information that I find in my sources that help me answer my Inquiry Questions:*	*I explain the reason why I think they are important and write personal comments:*

TAKING NOTES TOOL

Name _

Source(s) _ _ _ _ _ _ _ _ _ _ _ _ _ _ _ _ _ _

Inquiry Question/Path _ _ _ _ _ _ _ _ _ _ _

REFERENCE	DETAILS	COMMENTS
Source no. and location in the source:	I record details, ideas, or information that I find in my sources that help me answer my Inquiry Questions:	I explain the reason why I think they are important and write personal comments:

ODELL
EDUCATION

FORMING EVIDENCE-BASED CLAIMS RESEARCH TOOL

Name _____

Source(s) _ _ _ _ _ _ _ _ _ _ _ _ _ _

Inquiry Question:

SEARCHING FOR DETAILS

I read the sources closely and mark words and phrases that help me answer my question.

SELECTING DETAILS

I select words or phrases from my search that I think are the most important for answering my question. I write the reference next to each detail.

Detail 1 (Ref.:)	Detail 2 (Ref.:)	Detail 3 (Ref.:)

ANALYZING AND CONNECTING DETAILS

I reread parts of the texts and think about the meaning of the details and what they tell me about my question. Then I compare the details and explain the connections I see among them.

What I think about the details and how I connect them:

MAKING A CLAIM

I state a conclusion I have come to and can support with evidence from the texts after reading them closely.

My claim that answers my Inquiry Question:

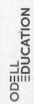
ODELL
EDUCATION

FORMING EVIDENCE-BASED CLAIMS RESEARCH TOOL

Name _____

Source(s) _

Inquiry Question:

SEARCHING FOR DETAILS	I read the sources closely and mark words and phrases that help me answer my question.

SELECTING DETAILS *I select words or phrases from my search that I think are the <u>most important</u> for answering my question. I write the <u>reference</u> next to each detail.*	**Detail 1 (Ref.:)**
	Detail 2 (Ref.:)
	Detail 3 (Ref.:)

| **ANALYZING AND CONNECTING DETAILS**

I reread parts of the texts and think about <u>the meaning of the details</u> and what they tell me about my question. Then I compare the details and explain <u>the connections</u> I see among them. | **What I think about the details and how I connect them:** |

| **MAKING A CLAIM**

I state a conclusion I have come to and can support with <u>evidence</u> from the texts after reading them closely. | **My claim that answers my Inquiry Question:** |

ODELL
EDUCATION

FORMING EVIDENCE-BASED CLAIMS RESEARCH TOOL

Name _   Source(s) _

Inquiry Question:

SEARCHING FOR DETAILS	I read the sources closely and mark words and phrases that help me answer my question.		
	Detail 1 (Ref.:)	Detail 2 (Ref.:)	Detail 3 (Ref.:)
SELECTING DETAILS *I select words or phrases from my search that I think are the <u>most important</u> for answering my question. I write the reference next to each detail.*			

ANALYZING AND CONNECTING DETAILS	What I think about the details and how I connect them:
ANALYZING AND CONNECTING DETAILS *I reread parts of the texts and think about <u>the meaning of the details</u> and what they tell me about my question. Then I compare the details and explain <u>the connections</u> I see among them.*	

MAKING A CLAIM	My claim that answers my Inquiry Question:
MAKING A CLAIM *I state a conclusion I have come to and can support with <u>evidence</u> from the texts after reading them closely.*	

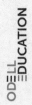
ODELL EDUCATION

FORMING EVIDENCE-BASED CLAIMS RESEARCH TOOL

Name _____

Source(s) _____

Inquiry Question:

SEARCHING FOR DETAILS

I read the sources closely and mark words and phrases that help me answer my question.

SELECTING DETAILS

I select words or phrases from my search that I think are the most important for answering my question. I write the reference next to each detail.

Detail 1 (Ref.:)	Detail 2 (Ref.:)	Detail 3 (Ref.:)

ANALYZING AND CONNECTING DETAILS

What I think about the details and how I connect them:

I reread parts of the texts and think about the meaning of the details and what they tell me about my question. Then I compare the details and explain the connections I see among them.

MAKING A CLAIM

My claim that answers my Inquiry Question:

I state a conclusion I have come to and can support with evidence from the texts after reading them closely.

ODELL EDUCATION

FORMING EVIDENCE-BASED CLAIMS RESEARCH TOOL

Name _____

Source(s) _____

Inquiry Question:

SEARCHING FOR DETAILS | I read the sources closely and mark words and phrases that help me answer my question.

SELECTING DETAILS

I select words or phrases from my search that I think are the most important for answering my question. I write the reference next to each detail.

Detail 1 (Ref.:)	Detail 2 (Ref.:)	Detail 3 (Ref.:)

ANALYZING AND CONNECTING DETAILS

I reread parts of the texts and think about the meaning of the details and what they tell me about my question. Then I compare the details and explain the connections I see among them.

What I think about the details and how I connect them:

MAKING A CLAIM

I state a conclusion I have come to and can support with evidence from the texts after reading them closely.

My claim that answers my Inquiry Question:

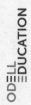

ODELL EDUCATION

ORGANIZING EVIDENCE-BASED CLAIMS RESEARCH TOOL (2 POINTS)

Name _ _ _ _ _ _ _ _ _ _ _ _ _ _   **Inquiry Question** _ _ _ _ _ _ _ _ _ _ _ _

CLAIM:

Point 1

A Supporting Evidence	B Supporting Evidence
(Reference:)	(Reference:)
C Supporting Evidence	D Supporting Evidence
(Reference:)	(Reference:)

Point 2

A Supporting Evidence	B Supporting Evidence
(Reference:)	(Reference:)
C Supporting Evidence	D Supporting Evidence
(Reference:)	(Reference:)

ODELL EDUCATION

ORGANIZING EVIDENCE-BASED CLAIMS RESEARCH TOOL (3 POINTS)

Name _____

Inquiry Question _____

CLAIM: _____

Point 1

A   Supporting Evidence

(Reference:)

B   Supporting Evidence

(Reference:)

C   Supporting Evidence

(Reference:)

Point 2

A   Supporting Evidence

(Reference:)

B   Supporting Evidence

(Reference:)

C   Supporting Evidence

(Reference:)

Point 3

A   Supporting Evidence

(Reference:)

B   Supporting Evidence

(Reference:)

C   Supporting Evidence

(Reference:)

ORGANIZING EVIDENCE-BASED CLAIMS RESEARCH TOOL (2 POINTS)

Name _   **Inquiry Question** _

CLAIM:

Point 1

A	Supporting Evidence	B	Supporting Evidence
(Reference:)		(Reference:)	
C	Supporting Evidence	D	Supporting Evidence
(Reference:)		(Reference:)	

Point 2

A	Supporting Evidence	B	Supporting Evidence
(Reference:)		(Reference:)	
C	Supporting Evidence	D	Supporting Evidence
(Reference:)		(Reference:)	

ODELL EDUCATION

ORGANIZING EVIDENCE-BASED CLAIMS RESEARCH TOOL (3 POINTS)

Name _ _ _ _ _ _ _ _ _ _ _ _ _ _ _ _ _ **Inquiry Question** _ _ _ _ _ _ _ _ _ _ _ _ _

CLAIM:

Point 1

| **A** Supporting Evidence |
| (Reference:) |
| **B** Supporting Evidence |
| (Reference:) |
| **C** Supporting Evidence |
| (Reference:) |

Point 2

| **A** Supporting Evidence |
| (Reference:) |
| **B** Supporting Evidence |
| (Reference:) |
| **C** Supporting Evidence |
| (Reference:) |

Point 3

| **A** Supporting Evidence |
| (Reference:) |
| **B** Supporting Evidence |
| (Reference:) |
| **C** Supporting Evidence |
| (Reference:) |

ODELL EDUCATION

FORMING EVIDENCE-BASED CLAIMS RESEARCH TOOL

Name _ Source(s) _

Inquiry Question:

SEARCHING FOR DETAILS	I read the sources closely and mark words and phrases that help me answer my question.		
SELECTING DETAILS *I select words or phrases from my search that I think are the <u>most important</u> for answering my question. I write the <u>reference next to each detail.</u>*	**Detail 1** (Ref.:)	**Detail 2** (Ref.:)	**Detail 3** (Ref.:)
ANALYZING AND CONNECTING DETAILS *I reread parts of the texts and think about the meaning of <u>the details</u> and what they tell me about my question. Then I compare the details and explain <u>the connections</u> I see among them.*	What I think about the details and how I connect them:		
MAKING A CLAIM *I state a conclusion I have come to and can support with <u>evidence</u> from the texts after reading them closely.*	My claim that answers my Inquiry Question:		

ODELL
EDUCATION

FORMING EVIDENCE-BASED CLAIMS RESEARCH TOOL

Name --

Inquiry Question:

Source(s) -------------------------------------

SEARCHING FOR DETAILS	I read the sources closely and mark words and phrases that help me answer my question.		
SELECTING DETAILS *I select words or phrases from my search that I think are the <u>most important</u> for answering my question. I write the reference next to each detail.*	**Detail 1** (Ref.:)	**Detail 2** (Ref.:)	**Detail 3** (Ref.:)
ANALYZING AND CONNECTING DETAILS *I reread parts of the texts and think about the meaning of the details and what they tell me about my question. Then I compare the details and explain the connections I see among them.*	What I think about the details and how I connect them:		
MAKING A CLAIM *I state a conclusion I have come to and can support with evidence from the texts after reading them closely.*	My claim that answers my Inquiry Question:		

ODELL
EDUCATION

TAKING NOTES TOOL

Name _

Source(s) _

Inquiry Question/Path _ _ _ _ _ _ _ _ _ _ _ _ _

REFERENCE	DETAILS	COMMENTS
Source no. and location in the source:	I record details, ideas, or information that I find in my sources that help me answer my Inquiry Questions:	I explain the reason why I think they are important and write personal comments:

ODELL EDUCATION

TAKING NOTES TOOL

Name _

Source(s) _ _ _ _ _ _ _ _ _ _ _ _ _ _ _ _ _ _ _

Inquiry Question/Path _ _ _ _ _ _ _ _ _ _ _ _ _

REFERENCE	DETAILS	COMMENTS
Source no. and location in the source:	I record details, ideas, or information that I find in my sources that help me answer my Inquiry Questions:	I explain the reason why I think they are important and write personal comments:

TAKING NOTES TOOL

Name _

Source(s) _

Inquiry Question/Path _ _ _ _ _ _ _ _ _ _ _ _ _

REFERENCE	DETAILS	COMMENTS
Source no. and location in the source:	I record details, ideas, or information that I find in my sources that help me answer my Inquiry Questions:	I explain the reason why I think they are important and write personal comments:

ODELL
EDUCATION

ORGANIZING EVIDENCE-BASED CLAIMS RESEARCH TOOL (2 POINTS)

Name _ _ _ _ _ _ _ _ _ _ _ _ _ _ _ _   Inquiry Question _ _ _ _ _ _ _ _ _ _

CLAIM:

Point 1

A   Supporting Evidence

(Reference:)

B   Supporting Evidence

(Reference:)

C   Supporting Evidence

(Reference:)

D   Supporting Evidence

(Reference:)

Point 2

A   Supporting Evidence

(Reference:)

B   Supporting Evidence

(Reference:)

C   Supporting Evidence

(Reference:)

D   Supporting Evidence

(Reference:)

ODELL EDUCATION

ORGANIZING EVIDENCE-BASED CLAIMS RESEARCH TOOL (3 POINTS)

Name _____

---------- **Inquiry Question** ----------

CLAIM:

Point 1	Point 2	Point 3
A Supporting Evidence	**A** Supporting Evidence	**A** Supporting Evidence
(Reference:)	(Reference:)	(Reference:)
B Supporting Evidence	**B** Supporting Evidence	**B** Supporting Evidence
(Reference:)	(Reference:)	(Reference:)
C Supporting Evidence	**C** Supporting Evidence	**C** Supporting Evidence
(Reference:)	(Reference:)	(Reference:)

AREA EVALUATION CHECKLIST

Date   **Name**   **Area of Investigation**

AREA EVALUATION CHECKLIST		√	COMMENTS
I. COHERENCE OF AREA *What is the Area of Investigation?*	The researcher can speak and write about the Area of Investigation in a way that makes sense to others and is clearly understood.		
II. SCOPE OF AREA *What do I need to know to gain an understanding of the Area of Investigation?*	The questions necessary to investigate for gaining an understanding require more than a quick review of easily accessed sources. The questions are reasonable enough so that the researcher is likely to find credible sources that address the issue in the time allotted for research.		
III. RELEVANCE OF AREA *How is this Area of Investigation related to a larger topic?*	The Area of Investigation is relevant to the larger topic.		
IV. INTEREST IN AREA *Why are you interested in this Area of Investigation?*	The researcher is able to communicate genuine interest in the Area of Investigation. Gaining an understanding of the area would be valuable for the student.		

In one or two sentences express the potential Area of Investigation in the form of a problem or overarching question:

RESEARCH EVALUATION CHECKLIST

Name _____ Area of Investigation _____ Date _____

RESEARCH EVALUATION CRITERIA CHECKLIST	√	COMMENTS
I. ADEQUACY AND SUFFICIENCY OF RESEARCH *The researcher's investigation follows the Area of Investigation and the information gathered is sufficient.*		
Adequacy of the research: The researcher's investigation is based on the Area of Investigation and the claims and information presented link directly to the Inquiry Questions.	☐	
Sufficiency of the answers: The answers formulated by the researcher based on his or her investigation are sufficient to cover the scope of each Inquiry Question.	☐	
Adequacy of the scope and focus of the research: No Inquiry Questions or Paths of the research seem irrelevant with respect to the Area of Investigation.	☐	
II. CREDIBILITY AND RICHNESS OF SOURCES *The sources gathered by the researcher are credible and rich.*		
Credibility of sources: The sources gathered by the researcher are credible.	☐	
Richness of sources: The researcher found a reasonable amount of rich sources that provide important information that is relevant to the inquiry.	☐	
III. RANGE OF PERSPECTIVES *The researcher has considered a wide range of perspectives.*		
Richness of perspectives: The researcher has considered and explored multiple perspectives.	☐	
Sufficiency of perspectives: No important perspective has been ignored.	☐	
Balance among perspectives: There is no overreliance on any one source or perspective.	☐	
IV. COHERENCE OF THE PERSPECTIVE *The evidence-based claims drawn from the analysis of the sources are coherent, sound, and supported.*		
Coherence of evidence-based claims: The evidence-based claims drawn from the analysis of the sources are coherent with respect to the Area of Investigation.	☐	
Soundness of evidence-based claims: The evidence-based claims demonstrate knowledge of and sound thinking about the Area of Investigation.	☐	
Support for evidence-based claims: The evidence-based claims are supported by quotations and examples from the texts.	☐	

ODELL EDUCATION

STUDENT RESEARCH LITERACY SKILLS AND HABITS CHECKLIST

	RESEARCH LITERACY SKILLS AND ACADEMIC HABITS	✔	Evidence Demonstrating the SKILLS AND HABITS
READING	1. **Identifying Relationships:** Notices important connections among details, ideas, and texts		
	2. **Making Inferences:** Draws sound conclusions from examining a text closely		
	3. **Summarizing:** Correctly explains what a text says about a topic		
	4. **Questioning:** Develops questions and lines of inquiry that lead to important ideas		
THINKING	5. **Recognizing Perspective:** Identifies and explains the author's view of the text's topic		
	6. **Evaluating Information:** Assesses the relevance and credibility of information in texts		
	7. **Forming Claims:** States a meaningful conclusion that is well supported by evidence from texts		
	8. **Using Evidence:** Uses well-chosen details from texts to explain and support claims; accurately paraphrases or quotes		
	9. **Organizing Ideas:** Organizes claims, supporting ideas, and evidence in a logical order		
	10. **Publishing:** Uses effective formatting and citations when paraphrasing, quoting, and listing sources		
	11. **Reflecting Critically:** Uses literacy concepts to discuss and evaluate personal and peer learning		
ACADEMIC HABITS	12. **Generating Ideas:** Generates and develops ideas, positions, products, and solutions to problems		
	13. **Organizing Work:** Maintains materials so that they can be used effectively and efficiently		
	14. **Completing Tasks:** Finishes short and extended tasks by established deadlines		
	15. **Understanding Purpose and Process:** Understands why and how a task should be accomplished		

General comments:

ODELL EDUCATION

BUILDING
EVIDENCE-BASED ARGUMENTS

DEVELOPING CORE LITERACY PROFICIENCIES

GRADE 6

"Energy Crossroads"

GOAL

In this unit you will develop your proficiency as a presenter of reasoned arguments. You will learn how to do the following:

1. Understand the background and key aspects of an important issue.
2. Look at various viewpoints on the issue.
3. Read the arguments of others closely and thoughtfully.
4. Develop your own view of the issue and take a stand about it.
5. Make and prove your case by using sound evidence and reasoning to support it.
6. Improve your writing so that others will clearly understand and appreciate your evidence-based argument—and think about the case you have made for it.

TOPIC

In this unit you will learn about how we make and use *energy*. You will learn about how natural gas can be taken from the ground to provide us with another source of energy. As you explore the topic further, you will discover that people do not all agree that this is a good idea. The complex process to extract the gas from the ground, called *hydraulic fracturing* or just *fracking*, raises many questions and leads to strong views, both for and against. Some people highlight the jobs and large amounts of energy the process produces. Others believe that the process might not be as safe as we think—and potentially harms our water. At first, you will try not to take a side as you learn about the topic and issues. Eventually, through careful research, discussion, and thinking, you will develop your own view, or perspective, and argue for a position that is supported by evidence and makes sense to you.

ACTIVITIES

You will begin the unit learning about the issue of using the fracking process to find natural gas. As you begin to understand the issue, you will explore the various perspectives on fracking. You will then read and analyze a few arguments. After analyzing arguments, you will develop your own position on the issue. Using your notes, you will plan an argument to defend your position. The unit finishes with a collaborate process you will use with your classmates to help you write and revise your final argumentative essay.

EVIDENCE-BASED ARGUMENTS TERMS

Issue:

an important aspect of human society for which there are many different opinions about what to think or do; many issues can be framed as a problem-based question

Relationship to issue:

a person's particular personal involvement with an issue, given his or her experience, education, occupation, socioeconomic-geographical status, interests, or other characteristics

Perspective:

how someone understands and views an issue based on his or her current relationship to it and analysis of the issue

Position:

someone's stance on what to do or think about a clearly defined issue based on his or her perspective and understanding of it; when writing an argumentative essay, one's position may be expressed as a thesis and is supported by a set of evidence-based claims

Evidence:

the topical and textual facts, events, and ideas from which the claims of an argument arise and which are cited to support the argument's position

Claim:

a personal conclusion about a text, topic, event, or idea

Evidence-based claim:

a personal conclusion that arises from and is supported by textual and topical evidence

BUILDING EVIDENCE-BASED ARGUMENTS LITERACY TOOLBOX

In *Building Evidence-Based Arguments*, you will continue to build your "literacy toolbox" by learning how to use the following handouts, tools and checklists organized in your Student Edition.

 TOOLS

In addition to using the handouts, you will learn how to use the following tools. You may also use tools from previous Core Proficiencies units:

Analyzing Details Tool

from the *Reading Closely* unit

Questioning Path Tool

from the *Reading Closely* unit

Forming Evidence-Based Claims Tool

from the *Making Evidence-Based Claims* unit

Organizing Evidence-Based Claims Tool

from the *Making Evidence-Based Claims* unit

Delineating Arguments Tool

This tool helps you identify and analyze components of an argument. You can use it to analyze other people's arguments or to help you develop your own.

Evaluating Arguments Tool

This tool helps you evaluate six characteristics of an argument (some you have seen in the Delineating Arguments Tool): the argument's issue, perspective, position or thesis, claims, evidence, and conclusions. You can also use this tool to rate how convincing the argument is overall.

HANDOUTS AND MODEL ARGUMENTS

To support your work with the texts and the tools, you will be able to use the following informational handouts. You may also use handouts from previous Core Proficiencies units:

Guiding Questions Handout

from the *Reading Closely* unit

Connecting Ideas Handout

from the *Research* unit

Evidence-Based Arguments Final Writing Task Handout

This handout gives you a detailed breakdown of the final argumentative essay.

Evidence-Based Arguments Terms

This handout defines the terms used in the unit to talk about and analyze arguments.

Model Arguments

These examples present familiar situations about which people take different positions. You can use these models to practice analyzing arguments.

CHECKLIST

You will also use this checklist throughout the unit to support peer- and self-review:

Building Evidence-Based Arguments Skills and Habits Checklist

This checklist presents and briefly describes the Literacy Skills and Habits you will be working on during the unit. You can use it to remind you of what you are trying to learn. You can also use it to reflect on what you have done when reading, discussing, or writing. It can help you give feedback to other students about their arguments. Your teacher may use it to let you know about your areas of strength and areas in which you need to improve.

Developing Core Literacy Proficiencies

BUILDING EVIDENCE-BASED ARGUMENTS UNIT TEXT SET

The following table lists the unit texts (organized by numbered text sets) that are used in the activities you will experience as you learn about argumentation. You will read some, but not all, of these texts, depending on decisions your teacher and students in your class make. Additional texts you can read to deepen your understanding are indicated with an *AT*.

These texts are accessible on the web for free without any login information, membership requirements, or purchase. Your teacher may provide you with copies of the texts you will read, or you may need to do an Internet search to find them. Because of the ever-changing nature of website addresses, links are not provided. You can locate these texts through web searches using the information provided. To find some of the texts, you may need to use online database portals (e.g., EBSCO, Gale) that are available to teachers and students through your state or district library systems.

TEXT	TITLE	AUTHOR	DATE	SOURCE/ PUBLISHER
Text Set 1: *Background Informational Texts*				
1.1	"How Much Energy Does the US Use"?	Alexis Madrigal	8/5/2013	*The Atlantic*
1.2	"The Story of Energy—Where Does Our Power Come From?"	LifeSquared	9/18/2012	LifeSquared.org
1.3	"History of Energy Use in the US"	Hobart King	NA	Geology.com
Text Set 2: *Additional Background Informational Texts*				
2.1	"What's Behind the Natural Gas Boom?"	Alexis Madrigal	8/21/2013	*The Atlantic*
2.2	"Energy Sources"	NA	NA	US Energy Information Administration— Energy Kids
2.3	"One Fracking Minute: An Animated Explainer on Hydraulic Fracturing"	Scott Tong and Matt Berger	12/7/2012	Marketplace.org
2.4	"Breaking Fuel from the Rock"	NA	NA	*National Geographic*
AT	"Natural Gas"	NA	1/10/2014	Grolier Online
AT	"Alternative Energy"	NA	1/10/2014	Grolier Online
AT	"Fracking Fury"	Janna Palliser	3/12/2014	Science Scope
AT	"Energy Resources"	NA	NA	*Geography 4 Kids*

AT	"Non-Renewable Energy"	NA	NA	SolarSchools.net
AT	"Natural Gas Basics"	NA	NA	US Energy Information Administration—Energy Kids
AT	"Natural Gas Usage"	Marcellus Shale Coalition	NA	Marcellus Shale Coalition.org
Text Set 3: *Political Cartoons*				
3.1	Fracking Political Cartoons	Multiple	NA	Cagle Cartoons.com
Text Set 4: *Seminal Arguments*				
4.1	"Understanding Fracking: Arguments For and Against Natural Gas Extraction"	Samantha Rae-Tuthill	9/9/2013	accuweather.com
4.2	"The Costs of Fracking"	Environment America Research and Policy Center	3/20/2012	EnvironmentAmerica.org
4.3	"Poverty and Fracking"	John Harpole	9/28/2013	DenverPost.com
4.4	"What the Frack? Natural Gas from Subterranean Shale Promises US Energy Independence—With Environmental Costs"	David Biello	3/30/2010	*Scientific American*
AT	"Why Cuomo Must Seize the Moment on Hydrofracking"	Ed Rendell	3/27/2013	*NY Daily News*
Text Set 5: *Contemporary Arguments*				
5.1	"Obama State of the Union: Safe Fracking Will Create 600K Jobs"	President Barack Obama	1/24/2012	Marcellus Drilling News
5.2	"Don't Frack New York"	NA	NA	Don'tfrackny.org
5.3	"Natural Gas from Shale: Unlocking Energy from Shale Rock Formations"	Chevron	6/2013	Chevron
5.4	"A New Day for North Dakota: The Fracking Miracle"	IER	6/19/2012	Institute for Energy Research
AT	"Renewables and Conservation Are Not Enough"	Power Worker's Union	3/9/2011	YouTube
AT	"Don't Let Extremists Undermine Fracking Boom"	Jack Rafuse	11/25/2013	The Hill.com

AT	"Truth about Hydraulic Fracking: Animation of Hydraulic Fracking"	Marathon Oil Corp	4/26/2012	YouTube
AT	"Natural Gas, Fueling an Economic Revolution"	Fareed Zakaria	3/29/2012	*Washington Post*
AT	"It's Time to Move America Beyond Oil"	Sierra Club	NA	Sierra Club
AT	"Is Fracking a Good Idea?"	NA	NA	US News Debate Club
AT	"Ban Fracking in Thousand Oaks"	NA	NA	CredoMobilize.com

BUILDING
EVIDENCE-BASED
ARGUMENTS

DEVELOPING CORE LITERACY
PROFICIENCIES

GRADE 6

Literacy Toolbox

CONNECTING IDEAS

USING TRANSITIONAL WORDS AND PHRASES

Transitional words and phrases create links between your ideas when you are speaking and writing. They help your audience understand the logic of your thoughts. When using transitional words, make sure that they are the right match for what you want to express. And remember, transition words work best when they are connecting two or more strong ideas that are clearly stated. Here is a list of transitional words and phrases that you can use for different purposes.

ADD RELATED INFORMATION	GIVE AN EXAMPLE OR ILLUSTRATE AN IDEA	MAKE SURE YOUR THINKING IS CLEARLY UNDERSTOOD	COMPARE IDEAS OR SHOW HOW IDEAS ARE SIMILAR	CONTRAST IDEAS OR SHOW HOW THEY ARE DIFFERENT
• furthermore • moreover • too • also • again • in addition • next • further • finally • and, or, nor	• to illustrate • to demonstrate • specifically • for instance • as an illustration • for example	• that is to say • in other words • to explain • i.e., (that is) • to clarify • to rephrase it • to put it another way	• in the same way • by the same token • similarly • in like manner • likewise • in similar fashion	• nevertheless • but • however • otherwise • on the contrary • in contrast • on the other hand

EXPLAIN HOW ONE THING CAUSES ANOTHER	EXPLAIN THE EFFECT OR RESULT OF SOMETHING	EXPLAIN YOUR PURPOSE	LIST RELATED INFORMATION	QUALIFY SOMETHING
• because • since • on account of • for that reason	• therefore • consequently • accordingly • thus • hence • as a result	• in order that • so that • to that end, to this end • for this purpose • for this reason	• First, second, third… • First, then, also, finally	• almost • nearly • probably • never • always • frequently • perhaps • maybe • although

BUILDING EVIDENCE-BASED ARGUMENTS—FINAL WRITING TASK

In this unit, you have been developing your skills as a presenter of reasoned arguments:

- Understanding the background and key aspects of an important issue
- Looking at various viewpoints on the issue
- Reading the arguments of others closely and thoughtfully
- Developing your own view of the issue and taking a position on it
- Making and proving your case by using sound evidence and reasoning to support it
- Improving your thinking and writing so that others will clearly understand and appreciate your evidence-based argument—and think about the case you have made for it

Your final writing assignment—the development of an evidence-based argumentative essay—will provide you with opportunities to use all of these related skills and to demonstrate your proficiency and growth in building evidence-based arguments. The assignment will also represent your final work in the Developing Core Literacy Proficiencies sequence and should demonstrate all that you have learned as a reader, thinker, and writer this year.

FINAL ASSIGNMENT

Developing, Writing, and Revising an Evidence-Based Argumentative Essay

Having read a collection of informational texts and arguments related to the unit's issue, you will develop a supported position on the issue. You will then plan, draft, and revise a multiparagraph essay that makes a case for your position. To do this, you will do the following:

1. Review the texts you have read, the tools you have completed, and the claims you have formed throughout the unit to determine the position you will take on the issue.
2. Write a paragraph that clearly states and explains your position—and the support you have found for it.
3. Read or reread arguments related to your position, looking for evidence you might use to support your argument.
4. Use a Delineating Arguments Tool to plan a multiparagraph essay that presents a series of claims, supported by evidence, to develop an argument in favor of your position.
5. Draft a multiparagraph essay that explains, develops, and supports your argumentative position—keeping in mind these criteria for this final writing assignment. Your essay should accomplish the following:
   ⇒ Present a convincing argument that comes from your understanding of the issue and a clear perspective and position.
   ⇒ Organize a set of claims in an order that explains and supports your position.
   ⇒ Use relevant and trustworthy evidence to support all claims and your overall position.
   ⇒ Represent the best thinking and writing you can do.

6. Use a collaborative process with other students to review and improve your draft in key areas:
   ⇒ The information and ideas that make up your argument
   ⇒ The organization (unity and logical sequence) of your argument
   ⇒ Your selection, use, and integration of supporting evidence (quotations, facts, statistics, references to other arguments, etc.)
   ⇒ The clarity of your writing—in areas identified by your teacher
7. Reflect on how well you have used Literacy Skills and Academic Habits throughout the unit and in developing your final written argument.

SKILLS AND HABITS TO BE DEMONSTRATED

As you become an expert on your issue and develop your evidence-based position and argument, think about demonstrating the Literacy Skills and Academic Habits listed in the following to the best of your ability. Your teacher will evaluate your work and determine your grade based on how well you demonstrate these skills and habits.

READ

Recognize Perspective: Identify and explain each author's view of the unit's issue.

Evaluate Information: Assess the relevance and credibility of information in texts about the issue.

Delineate Arguments: Identify and analyze the claims, evidence, and reasoning of arguments related to the issue.

DEVELOP ACADEMIC HABITS

Remain Open to New Ideas: Ask questions of others rather than arguing for your own ideas or opinions.

Qualify Your Views: Explain and change your ideas in response to thinking from others.

Revise: Rethink your position and refine your writing based on feedback from others.

Reflect Critically: Discuss and evaluate your learning, using the criteria that describe the Literacy Skills and Academic Habits you have been developing.

WRITE

Form Claims: State meaningful positions and conclusions that are well supported by evidence from texts you have examined.

Use Evidence: Use well-chosen details from the texts to support your position and claims. Accurately paraphrase or quote what the authors say in the texts.

Use Logic: Argue for your position through a logical sequence of related claims and supporting evidence.

Organize Ideas: Organize your argument, supporting claims, and evidence in an order that makes sense to others.

Use Language: Write clearly so others can understand your position, claims, and supporting ideas.

Use Conventions: Correctly use sentence elements, punctuation, and spelling to produce clear writing.

Publish: Correctly use, format, and cite textual evidence to support your argument.

NOTE

These skills and habits are also listed on the *Student Literacy Skills and Academic Habits Checklist*, which you can use to assess your work and the work of other students.

ODELL
EDUCATION

QUESTIONING PATH TOOL

Text 1.1—"How Much Energy Does the US Use?" Animated Video

APPROACHING: *I determine my reading purposes and take note of key information about the text. I identify the LIPS domain(s) that will guide my initial reading.*

QUESTIONING: *I use Guiding Questions to help me investigate the text (from the **Guiding Questions Handout**).*

ANALYZING: *I question further to connect and analyze the details I find (from the **Guiding Questions Handout**).*

1. What new ideas or information do I find in the text?

2. What claims do I find in the text?

DEEPENING: *I consider the questions of others.*

3. The video begins with the question "How much energy does the US use in a year?" What information does it present to answer this question?

4. "More than 80% of energy used in the US comes from" which three sources? What does this claim mean in terms of our current and future use of energy?

EXTENDING: *I pose my own questions.*

5. What evidence does this text provide that builds my understanding of the issue of energy use and production in the United States?

QUESTIONING PATH TOOL

Text 1.2—"The Story of Energy" Animated Video

APPROACHING: *I determine my reading purposes and take note of key information about the text. I identify the LIPS domain(s) that will guide my initial reading.*

QUESTIONING: *I use Guiding Questions to help me investigate the text (from the Guiding Questions Handout).*

ANALYZING: *I question further to connect and analyze the details I find (from the Guiding Questions Handout).*

1. What new ideas or information do I find in the text?

2. What claims do I find in the text?

DEEPENING: *I consider the questions of others.*

3. What reasons does the narrator give for focusing on gas use in the video? How do these reasons relate to US energy use and production?

4. How might the energy story for the United Kingdom be similar and different to the story for the United States?

5. What claims does the video make about the need for renewable sources of energy? What evidence supports these claims?

EXTENDING: *I pose my own questions.*

6. What evidence does this text provide that builds my understanding of the issue of energy use and production in the United States?

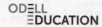
ODELL EDUCATION

QUESTIONING PATH TOOL

Text 1.3—"The Story of Energy" Animated Video

APPROACHING: *I determine my reading purposes and take note of key information about the text. I identify the LIPS domain(s) that will guide my initial reading.*

QUESTIONING: *I use Guiding Questions to help me investigate the text (from the **Guiding Questions Handout**).*

ANALYZING: *I question further to connect and analyze the details I find (from the **Guiding Questions Handout**).*

1. What new ideas or information do I find in the text?

2. What claims do I find in the text?

DEEPENING: *I consider the questions of others.*

3. For any energy source described in the text, what is stated regarding its history?

4. For any energy source described in the text, how has its use changed over time?

5. What connections does the text make between energy sources and energy demands?

EXTENDING: *I pose my own questions.*

6. What evidence does this text provide that builds my understanding of the issue of energy use and production in the United States?

ANALYZING DETAILS TOOL

Name _____

Text _____

Reading purpose:

A question I have about the text:

SEARCHING FOR DETAILS

I read the text closely and mark words and phrases that help me think about my question.

SELECTING DETAILS

I select words or phrases from my search that I think are the **most important** in thinking about my question.

Detail 1 (Ref.:)	Detail 2 (Ref.:)	Detail 3 (Ref.:)

ANALYZING DETAILS

I reread parts of the text and think about the **meaning of the details** and what they tell me about my question.

What I think about detail 1:	What I think about detail 2:	What I think about detail 3:

CONNECTING DETAILS

I compare the details and explain the connections I see among them.

How I connect the details:

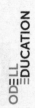
ODELL EDUCATION

ANALYZING DETAILS TOOL

Name _ _ _ _ _ _ _ _ _ _ _ _ _ _ _ _ _ **Text** _ _ _ _ _ _ _ _ _ _ _ _ _ _ _ _ _

Reading purpose:

A question I have about the text:

SEARCHING FOR DETAILS	I read the text closely and mark words and phrases that help me think about my question.

SELECTING DETAILS I select words or phrases from my search that I think are the most important in thinking about my question.	**Detail 1 (Ref.:)**	**Detail 2 (Ref.:)**	**Detail 3 (Ref.:)**

ANALYZING DETAILS I reread parts of the text and think about the meaning of the details and what they tell me about my question.	**What I think about detail 1:**	**What I think about detail 2:**	**What I think about detail 3:**

CONNECTING DETAILS I compare the details and explain the connections I see among them.	**How I connect the details:**

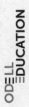

ODELL
EDUCATION

ANALYZING DETAILS TOOL

Name _ _ _ _ _ _ _ _ _ _ _ _ _ _ Text _ _ _ _ _ _ _ _ _ _ _ _ _ _ _ _ _

Reading purpose:

A question I have about the text:

SEARCHING FOR DETAILS	I read the text closely and mark words and phrases that help me think about my question.		
SELECTING DETAILS I select words or phrases from my search that I think are the most important in thinking about my question.	Detail 1 (Ref.:)	Detail 2 (Ref.:)	Detail 3 (Ref.:)
ANALYZING DETAILS I reread parts of the text and think about the meaning of the details and what they tell me about my question.	What I think about detail 1:	What I think about detail 2:	What I think about detail 3:
CONNECTING DETAILS I compare the details and explain the connections I see among them.	How I connect the details:		

FORMING EVIDENCE-BASED CLAIMS TOOL (EBA)

Name _____   Text _____

A question I have about the text:

SEARCHING FOR DETAILS

I read the text closely and mark words and phrases that help me answer my question.

Detail 1 (Ref.:)	Detail 2 (Ref.:)	Detail 3 (Ref.:)

SELECTING DETAILS

I select words or phrases from my search that I think are the most important for answering my question. I write the reference next to each detail.

ANALYZING DETAILS

What I think about detail 1:	What I think about detail 2:	What I think about detail 3:

I reread parts of the texts and think about the meaning of the details and what they tell me about my question. Then I compare the details and explain the connections I see among them.

CONNECTING DETAILS

How I connect the details:

I compare the details and explain the connections I see among them.

MAKING A CLAIM

My claim about the text:

I state a conclusion I have come to and can support with evidence from the text after reading it closely.

ODELL EDUCATION

FORMING EVIDENCE-BASED CLAIMS TOOL (EBA)

Name _ _ _ _ _ _ _ _ _ _ _ _ _ _   Text _ _ _ _ _ _ _ _ _ _ _ _ _ _

A question I have about the text:

SEARCHING FOR DETAILS

I read the text closely and mark words and phrases that help me answer my question.

SELECTING DETAILS	Detail 1 (Ref.:)	Detail 2 (Ref.:)	Detail 3 (Ref.:)
I select words or phrases from my search that I think are the most important for answering my question. I write the reference next to each detail.			

ANALYZING DETAILS

ANALYZING DETAILS	What I think about detail 1:	What I think about detail 2:	What I think about detail 3:
I reread parts of the texts and think about the meaning of the details and what they tell me about my question. Then I compare the details and explain the connections I see among them.			

CONNECTING DETAILS

CONNECTING DETAILS	How I connect the details:
I compare the details and explain the connections I see among them.	

MAKING A CLAIM

MAKING A CLAIM	My claim about the text:
I state a conclusion I have come to and can support with evidence from the text after reading it closely.	

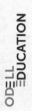

ODELL EDUCATION

FORMING EVIDENCE-BASED CLAIMS TOOL (EBA)

Name _____   Text _____

A question I have about the text:

SEARCHING FOR DETAILS

I read the text closely and mark words and phrases that help me answer my question.

SELECTING DETAILS	**Detail 1 (Ref.:)**	**Detail 2 (Ref.:)**	**Detail 3 (Ref.:)**
I select words or phrases from my search that I think are the <u>most</u> <u>important</u> for answering my question. I write the <u>reference</u> next to each detail.			

ANALYZING DETAILS

ANALYZING DETAILS	**What I think about detail 1:**	**What I think about detail 2:**	**What I think about detail 3:**
I reread parts of the texts and think about the meaning of the details and what they tell me about my question. Then I compare the details and explain <u>the connections</u> I see among them.			

CONNECTING DETAILS

CONNECTING DETAILS	**How I connect the details:**
I compare the details and explain <u>the connections</u> I see among them.	

MAKING A CLAIM

MAKING A CLAIM	**My claim about the text:**
I state a conclusion I have come to and can support with <u>evidence</u> from the text after reading it closely.	

ODELL
EDUCATION

QUESTIONING PATH TOOL

Text 2.1—"What's Behind the Natural Gas Boom?" Animated Video

APPROACHING: *I determine my reading purposes and take note of key information about the text. I identify the LIPS domain(s) that will guide my initial reading.*

QUESTIONING: *I use Guiding Questions to help me investigate the text (from the **Guiding Questions Handout**).*

ANALYZING: *I question further to connect and analyze the details I find (from the **Guiding Questions Handout**).*

1. What new ideas or information do I find in the text?

2. What claims do I find in the text?

DEEPENING: *I consider the questions of others.*

3. What is *shale gas*? How have new methods of extracting natural gas from shale changed the production and use of natural gas in the United States?

4. What percentage of natural gas production in the United States now comes from shale gas? What does this mean in terms of our dependence on this method of production and its impacts?

EXTENDING: *I pose my own questions.*

5. What evidence does this text provide that builds my understanding of the issue of energy use and production in the United States?

ODELL EDUCATION

QUESTIONING PATH TOOL

Text 2.2—Energy Sources Website

APPROACHING: *I determine my reading purposes and take note of key information about the text. I identify the LIPS domain(s) that will guide my initial reading.*

QUESTIONING: *I use Guiding Questions to help me investigate the text (from the Guiding Questions Handout).*

ANALYZING: *I question further to connect and analyze the details I find (from the Guiding Questions Handout).*

1. What new ideas or information do I find in the text?

2. What claims do I find in the text?

DEEPENING: *I consider the questions of others.*

3. For natural gas (or any of the selected sources of energy), how is it primarily produced and used to make energy?

4. For natural gas (or any of the selected sources of energy), what are the potential effects on the environment?

EXTENDING: *I pose my own questions.*

5. What evidence does this text provide that builds my understanding of the issue of energy use and production in the United States?

FORMING EVIDENCE-BASED CLAIMS TOOL (EBA)

Name _____ **Text** --------------------------

A question I have about the text:

SEARCHING FOR DETAILS

I read the text closely and mark words and phrases that help me answer my question.

SELECTING DETAILS

I select words or phrases from my search that I think are the most important for answering my question. I write the reference next to each detail.

Detail 1 (Ref.:)	Detail 2 (Ref.:)	Detail 3 (Ref.:)

ANALYZING DETAILS

I reread parts of the texts and think about the meaning of the details and what they tell me about my question. Then I compare the details and explain the connections I see among them.

What I think about detail 1:	What I think about detail 2:	What I think about detail 3:

CONNECTING DETAILS

I compare the details and explain the connections I see among them.

How I connect the details:

MAKING A CLAIM

I state a conclusion I have come to and can support with evidence from the text after reading it closely.

My claim about the text:

ODELL EDUCATION

FORMING EVIDENCE-BASED CLAIMS TOOL (EBA)

Name _ _ _ _ _ _ _ _ _ _ _ _ _ _ Text _ _ _ _ _ _ _ _ _ _ _ _ _ _ _ _

A question I have about the text:

SEARCHING FOR DETAILS I read the text closely and mark words and phrases that help me answer my question.

SELECTING DETAILS

I select words or phrases from my search that I think are the <u>most important</u> for answering my question. I write the <u>reference</u> next to each detail.

Detail 1 (Ref.:)	Detail 2 (Ref.:)	Detail 3 (Ref.:)

ANALYZING DETAILS

I reread parts of the texts and <u>think</u> about the meaning of the details and what they tell me about my question. Then I compare the details and explain the connections I see among them.

What I think about detail 1:	What I think about detail 2:	What I think about detail 3:

CONNECTING DETAILS

I compare the details and explain the <u>connections</u> I see among them.

How I connect the details:

MAKING A CLAIM

I state a conclusion I have come to and can support with evidence from the text after reading it closely.

My claim about the text:

ODELL
EDUCATION

QUESTIONING PATH TOOL

Name: _____ **Text:** _____

APPROACHING: *I determine my reading purposes and take note of key information about the text. I identify the LIPS domain(s) that will guide my initial reading.*

Purpose:

Key information:

LIPS domain(s):

QUESTIONING: *I use Guiding Questions to help me investigate the text (from the **Guiding Questions Handout**).*

1.

2.

ANALYZING: *I question further to connect and analyze the details I find (from the **Guiding Questions Handout**).*

1.

2.

DEEPENING: *I consider the questions of others.*

1.

2.

3.

EXTENDING: *I pose my own questions.*

1.

2.

ODELL EDUCATION

QUESTIONING PATH TOOL

Name: _____ **Text:** _____

APPROACHING:
I determine my reading purposes and take note of key information about the text. I identify the LIPS domain(s) that will guide my initial reading.

Purpose:

Key information:

LIPS domain(s):

QUESTIONING: *I use Guiding Questions to help me investigate the text (from the **Guiding Questions Handout**).*

1.

2.

ANALYZING: *I question further to connect and analyze the details I find (from the **Guiding Questions Handout**).*

1.

2.

DEEPENING: *I consider the questions of others.*

1.

2.

3.

EXTENDING: *I pose my own questions.*

1.

2.

FORMING EVIDENCE-BASED CLAIMS TOOL (EBA)

Name _____

Text _____

A question I have about the text:

_____

SEARCHING FOR DETAILS

I read the text closely and mark words and phrases that help me answer my question.

SELECTING DETAILS

I select words or phrases from my search that I think are the most important for answering my question. I write the reference next to each detail.

Detail 1 (Ref.:)	Detail 2 (Ref.:)	Detail 3 (Ref.:)

ANALYZING DETAILS

I reread parts of the texts and think about the meaning of the details and what they tell me about my question. Then I compare the details and explain the connections I see among them.

What I think about detail 1:	What I think about detail 2:	What I think about detail 3:

CONNECTING DETAILS

I compare the details and explain the connections I see among them.

How I connect the details:

_____

MAKING A CLAIM

I state a conclusion I have come to and can support with evidence from the text after reading it closely.

My claim about the text:

_____

ODELL EDUCATION

ORGANIZING EVIDENCE-BASED CLAIMS TOOL (2 POINTS)

Name _ _ _ _ _ _ _ _ _ _ _ _ _ _ _ _   Text _ _ _ _ _ _ _ _ _ _ _ _ _ _ _ _

CLAIM:

Point 1

A Supporting Evidence

B Supporting Evidence

(Reference:)

(Reference:)

C Supporting Evidence

D Supporting Evidence

(Reference:)

(Reference:)

Point 2

A Supporting Evidence

B Supporting Evidence

(Reference:)

(Reference:)

C Supporting Evidence

D Supporting Evidence

(Reference:)

(Reference:)

ODELL EDUCATION

ORGANIZING EVIDENCE-BASED CLAIMS TOOL (3 POINTS)

Name _ _ _ _ _ _ _ _ _ _ _ _ _ _ _ _ _   Text _ _ _ _ _ _ _ _ _ _ _ _ _ _ _ _

CLAIM:

Point 1	Point 2	Point 3
A Supporting Evidence	**A** Supporting Evidence	**A** Supporting Evidence
(Reference:)	(Reference:)	(Reference:)
B Supporting Evidence	**B** Supporting Evidence	**B** Supporting Evidence
(Reference:)	(Reference:)	(Reference:)
C Supporting Evidence	**C** Supporting Evidence	**C** Supporting Evidence
(Reference:)	(Reference:)	(Reference:)

ODELL EDUCATION

QUESTIONING PATH TOOL

Name: _____ **Text:** _____

APPROACHING: *I determine my reading purposes and take note of key information about the text. I identify the LIPS domain(s) that will guide my initial reading.*

Purpose:

Key information:

LIPS domain(s):

QUESTIONING: *I use Guiding Questions to help me investigate the text (from the **Guiding Questions Handout**).*

1.

2.

ANALYZING: *I question further to connect and analyze the details I find (from the **Guiding Questions Handout**).*

1.

2.

DEEPENING: *I consider the questions of others.*

1.

2.

3.

EXTENDING: *I pose my own questions.*

1.

2.

DELINEATING ARGUMENTS TOOL

Name - - - - - - - - - - Topic - - - - - - - - - -

ISSUE	
PERSPECTIVE	
POSITION	

CLAIM 1		CLAIM 2		CLAIM 3	
	Supporting evidence:		Supporting evidence:		Supporting evidence:

ODELL EDUCATION

DELINEATING ARGUMENTS TOOL

Name _____

Topic _____

ISSUE	

PERSPECTIVE	

POSITION	

CLAIM 1	
	Supporting evidence:

CLAIM 2	
	Supporting evidence:

CLAIM 3	
	Supporting evidence:

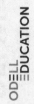
ODELL
EDUCATION

DELINEATING ARGUMENTS TOOL

Name _ _ _ _ _ _ _ _ _ _ _ _ _ Topic _ _ _ _ _ _ _

ISSUE

PERSPECTIVE

POSITION

CLAIM 1

Supporting evidence:

CLAIM 2

Supporting evidence:

CLAIM 3

Supporting evidence:

ODELL EDUCATION

DELINEATING ARGUMENTS TOOL

Name _ _ _ _ _ _ _ _ _ _ _ _ _ _ _ _ _ _

Topic _ _ _ _ _ _ _ _ _ _ _ _ _ _ _ _

ISSUE	

PERSPECTIVE	

POSITION	

CLAIM 1	
	Supporting evidence:

CLAIM 2	
	Supporting evidence:

CLAIM 3	
	Supporting evidence:

QUESTIONING PATH TOOL

Text 4.2—"The Costs of Fracking"

APPROACHING: *I determine my reading purposes and take note of key information about the text. I identify the LIPS domain(s) that will guide my initial reading.*	
QUESTIONING: *I use Guiding Questions to help me investigate the text (from the **Guiding Questions Handout**).*	
ANALYZING: *I question further to connect and analyze the details I find (from the **Guiding Questions Handout**).*	1. What seems to be the authors' attitude or point of view (based on their relationship to the issue)? 2. What do I notice about how the text is organized or sequenced? 3. What claims do I find in the text? 4. What evidence supports the claims in the text and what is left uncertain or unsupported? 5. In what ways are ideas and claims linked together in the text?
DEEPENING: *I consider the questions of others.*	6. Which sentences best communicate the Environment America's position about fracking? 7. The authors bold certain sentences and headings in the text. What does this bolded text communicate to the reader? 8. What elements of the argument do the bolded sections represent? 9. How does the bolded text help develop and support the authors' position? 10. How does one of these bolded sentences relate to the authors' overall argument, and what specific evidence do they offer for support?
EXTENDING: *I pose my own questions.*	11. What evidence does this text provide that builds my understanding of the issue of hydraulic fracturing (fracking) in the United States?

ODELL
EDUCATION

DELINEATING ARGUMENTS TOOL

Name _ _ _ _ _ _ _ _ _ _ _ _   **Topic** _ _ _ _ _ _ _ _ _ _ _ _

ISSUE

PERSPECTIVE

POSITION

CLAIM 1

Supporting evidence:

CLAIM 2

Supporting evidence:

CLAIM 3

Supporting evidence:

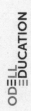

QUESTIONING PATH TOOL

Text 4.3: "Poverty and Fracking"

APPROACHING: *I determine my reading purposes and take note of key information about the text. I identify the LIPS domain(s) that will guide my initial reading.*	
QUESTIONING: *I use Guiding Questions to help me investigate the text (from the **Guiding Questions Handout**).*	
ANALYZING: *I question further to connect and analyze the details I find (from the **Guiding Questions Handout**).*	1. What do I learn about the author and the purpose for writing the text? 2. How does the author's perspective influence his presentation of ideas or arguments? 3. What evidence supports the claims in the text and what is left uncertain or unsupported?
DEEPENING: *I consider the questions of others.*	4. What is Harpole's position on hydraulic fracturing? Does he state it, and if so, where? 5. What is "the human side of the story" and why does Harpole decide to tell it? What is the connection he tries to make between his mom's utility bills and fracking? 6. Which evidence that Harpole cites seems most solid and convincing? What evidence seems more questionable?
EXTENDING: *I pose my own questions.*	7. What evidence does this text provide that builds my understanding of the issue of energy and fracking policy in the United States?

ODELL
EDUCATION

DELINEATING ARGUMENTS TOOL

Name _____   **Topic**

ISSUE	

PERSPECTIVE	

POSITION	

CLAIM 1		CLAIM 2		CLAIM 3	
	Supporting evidence:		Supporting evidence:		Supporting evidence:

ORGANIZING EVIDENCE-BASED CLAIMS TOOL (2 POINTS)

Name _ _ _ _ _ _ _ _ _ _ _ _ _ Text _ _ _ _ _ _ _ _ _ _ _ _ _ _ _ _ _

CLAIM:

Point 1

A	Supporting Evidence	B	Supporting Evidence

(Reference:) (Reference:)

C	Supporting Evidence	D	Supporting Evidence

(Reference:) (Reference:)

Point 2

A	Supporting Evidence	B	Supporting Evidence

(Reference:) (Reference:)

C	Supporting Evidence	D	Supporting Evidence

(Reference:) (Reference:)

ODELL EDUCATION

ORGANIZING EVIDENCE-BASED CLAIMS TOOL (3 POINTS)

Name _ _ _ _ _ _ _ _ _ _ _ _ _ _ Text _

CLAIM:

Point 1		Point 2		Point 3	
A	Supporting Evidence	**A**	Supporting Evidence	**A**	Supporting Evidence
(Reference:	**)**	**(Reference:**	**)**	**(Reference:**	**)**
B	Supporting Evidence	**B**	Supporting Evidence	**B**	Supporting Evidence
(Reference:	**)**	**(Reference:**	**)**	**(Reference:**	**)**
C	Supporting Evidence	**C**	Supporting Evidence	**C**	Supporting Evidence
(Reference:	**)**	**(Reference:**	**)**	**(Reference:**	**)**

EVALUATING ARGUMENTS TOOL

As you read and delineate the argument, think about each of the **elements** and their **guiding evaluation questions**. Rate each element as:

? a **questionable** part or weakness of the argument   ✔ a reasonable or **acceptable** part of the argument   **+** a **strength** of the argument

ELEMENTS	EVALUATING AN ARGUMENT: GUIDING QUESTIONS	?	✔	+	TEXT-BASED OBSERVATIONS
Issue	• How clearly is the issue presented and explained? • How accurate and current is the explanation of the issue?				
Perspective	• What is the author's relationship to the issue? What is the author's purpose for the argument? • What are the author's background and credentials relative to the issue? • What is the author's viewpoint or attitude about the issue? How reasonable is this perspective?				
Position	• How clearly is the author's position presented and explained? • How well is the position connected to the claims and evidence of the argument?				
Claims	• How clearly are the argument's claims explained and connected to the position? • Are the claims supported with evidence? • How well are the claims linked together into an argument?				
Evidence	• Does the supporting evidence come from a trustworthy source? Is it believable? • Is there enough evidence to make the argument convincing?				
Conclusions	• How logical and reasonable are the conclusions drawn by the author? • How well do the argument's conclusions or suggestions address the issue and align with the position?				
Convincing Argument	• How do the author's overall perspective and position on the issue compare with others? With my own? • Does the argument make sense to me? Do I agree with its claims? Am I convinced?				
Comments:					

ODELL
EDUCATION

EVALUATING ARGUMENTS TOOL

As you read and delineate the argument, think about each of the **elements** and their **guiding evaluation questions**. Rate each element as:

? a **questionable** part or weakness of the argument   **✔** a reasonable or **acceptable** part of the argument   **+** a **strength** of the argument

ELEMENTS	EVALUATING AN ARGUMENT: GUIDING QUESTIONS	?	✔	+	TEXT-BASED OBSERVATIONS
Issue	• How clearly is the issue presented and explained? • How accurate and current is the explanation of the issue?				
Perspective	• What is the author's relationship to the issue? What is the author's purpose for the argument? • What are the author's background and credentials relative to the issue? • What is the author's viewpoint or attitude about the issue? How reasonable is this perspective?				
Position	• How clearly is the author's position presented and explained? • How well is the position connected to the claims and evidence of the argument?				
Claims	• How clearly are the argument's claims explained and connected to the position? • Are the claims supported with evidence? • How well are the claims linked together into an argument?				
Evidence	• Does the supporting evidence come from a trustworthy source? Is it believable? • Is there enough evidence to make the argument convincing?				
Conclusions	• How logical and reasonable are the conclusions drawn by the author? • How well do the argument's conclusions or suggestions address the issue and align with the position?				
Convincing Argument	• How do the author's overall perspective and position on the issue compare with others? With my own? • Does the argument make sense to me? Do I agree with its claims? Am I convinced?				
Comments:					

DELINEATING ARGUMENTS TOOL

Name _ _ _ _ _ _ _ _ _ _ _ _ _ Topic

ISSUE	

PERSPECTIVE	

POSITION	

CLAIM 1	CLAIM 2	CLAIM 3
Supporting evidence:	**Supporting evidence:**	**Supporting evidence:**

DELINEATING ARGUMENTS TOOL

Name _ Topic _

ISSUE	

PERSPECTIVE	

POSITION	

CLAIM 1	CLAIM 2	CLAIM 3
Supporting evidence:	Supporting evidence:	Supporting evidence:

ORGANIZING EVIDENCE-BASED CLAIMS TOOL (2 POINTS)

Name _

Text _

CLAIM:

Point 1

A Supporting Evidence

(Reference:)

B Supporting Evidence

(Reference:)

C Supporting Evidence

(Reference:)

D Supporting Evidence

(Reference:)

Point 2

A Supporting Evidence

(Reference:)

B Supporting Evidence

(Reference:)

C Supporting Evidence

(Reference:)

D Supporting Evidence

(Reference:)

ODELL EDUCATION

ORGANIZING EVIDENCE-BASED CLAIMS TOOL (3 POINTS)

Name _ _ _ _ _ _ _ _ _   Text _ _ _ _ _ _ _ _ _

CLAIM:

Point 1

A   Supporting Evidence

(Reference:

B   Supporting Evidence

(Reference:

C   Supporting Evidence

(Reference:

Point 2

A   Supporting Evidence

(Reference:)

B   Supporting Evidence

(Reference:)

C   Supporting Evidence

(Reference:)

Point 3

A   Supporting Evidence

(Reference:)

B   Supporting Evidence

(Reference:)

C   Supporting Evidence

(Reference:)

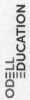
ODELL EDUCATION

DELINEATING ARGUMENTS TOOL

Name _ _ _ _ _ _ _ _ _ _ _ Topic _

ISSUE

PERSPECTIVE

POSITION

CLAIM 1

Supporting evidence:

CLAIM 2

Supporting evidence:

CLAIM 3

Supporting evidence:

ORGANIZING EVIDENCE-BASED CLAIMS TOOL (2 POINTS)

Name _ _ _ _ _ _ _ _ _ _ _ _ _ Text _ _ _ _ _ _ _ _ _ _ _ _ _

CLAIM:

Point 1

A	Supporting Evidence

(Reference:)

B	Supporting Evidence

(Reference:)

C	Supporting Evidence

(Reference:)

D	Supporting Evidence

(Reference:)

Point 2

A	Supporting Evidence

(Reference:)

B	Supporting Evidence

(Reference:)

C	Supporting Evidence

(Reference:)

D	Supporting Evidence

(Reference:)

ODELL EDUCATION

ORGANIZING EVIDENCE-BASED CLAIMS TOOL (3 POINTS)

Name _ _ _ _ _ _ _ _ _ _ _ _ Text _ _ _ _ _ _ _ _ _ _ _ _ _ _ _ _ _

CLAIM:

Point 1		Point 2		Point 3	
A Supporting Evidence		**A** Supporting Evidence		**A** Supporting Evidence	
(Reference:)		(Reference:)		(Reference:)	
B Supporting Evidence		**B** Supporting Evidence		**B** Supporting Evidence	
(Reference:)		(Reference:)		(Reference:)	
C Supporting Evidence		**C** Supporting Evidence		**C** Supporting Evidence	
(Reference:)		(Reference:)		(Reference:)	

DELINEATING ARGUMENTS TOOL

Name _ _ _ _ _ _ _ _ _ _ _ _ _ _ _ _ Topic _ _ _ _ _ _ _ _ _ _ _ _ _ _ _ _

ISSUE

PERSPECTIVE

POSITION

CLAIM 1	CLAIM 2	CLAIM 3
Supporting evidence:	Supporting evidence:	Supporting evidence:

ORGANIZING EVIDENCE-BASED CLAIMS TOOL (2 POINTS)

Name _____   Text _____

CLAIM:

Point 1

A Supporting Evidence

B Supporting Evidence

(Reference:)   (Reference:)

C Supporting Evidence

D Supporting Evidence

(Reference:)   (Reference:)

Point 2

A Supporting Evidence

B Supporting Evidence

(Reference:)   (Reference:)

C Supporting Evidence

D Supporting Evidence

(Reference:)   (Reference:)

ODELL EDUCATION

ORGANIZING EVIDENCE-BASED CLAIMS TOOL (3 POINTS)

Name _ _ _ _ _ _ _ _ _ _ Text _ _ _ _ _ _ _ _ _ _

CLAIM:

Point 1

A   Supporting Evidence

(Reference:)

B   Supporting Evidence

(Reference:)

C   Supporting Evidence

(Reference:)

Point 2

A   Supporting Evidence

(Reference:)

B   Supporting Evidence

(Reference:)

C   Supporting Evidence

(Reference:)

Point 3

A   Supporting Evidence

(Reference:)

B   Supporting Evidence

(Reference:)

C   Supporting Evidence

(Reference:)

BUILDING EVIDENCE-BASED ARGUMENTS LITERACY SKILLS AND ACADEMIC HABITS CHECKLIST

	EVIDENCE-BASED ARGUMENTS LITERACY SKILLS AND ACADEMIC HABITS	✔	EVIDENCE DEMONSTRATING THE SKILLS AND HABITS
READING	1. **Recognizing Perspective:** Identifies and explains the author's view of the text's topic		
	2. **Evaluating Information:** Assesses the relevance and credibility of information in texts		
	3. **Delineating Argumentation:** Identifies and analyzes the claims, evidence, and reasoning in arguments		
ACADEMIC HABITS	4. **Remaining Open:** Asks questions of others rather than arguing for a personal idea or opinion		
	5. **Qualifying Views:** Explains and changes ideas in response to thinking from others		
	6. **Revising:** Rethinks ideas and refines work based on feedback from others		
	7. **Reflecting Critically:** Uses literacy concepts to discuss and evaluate personal and peer learning		
WRITING SKILLS	8. **Forming Claims:** States a meaningful position that is well supported by evidence from texts		
	9. **Using Evidence:** Uses well-chosen details from texts to explain and support claims; accurately paraphrases or quotes		
	10. **Organizing Ideas:** Organizes claims, supporting ideas, and evidence in a logical order		
	11. **Using Language:** Writes clearly so others can understand claims and ideas		
	12. **Using Conventions:** Correctly uses sentence elements, punctuation, and spelling to produce clear writing		
	13. **Publishing:** Correctly uses, formats, and cites textual evidence to support claims		
	General comments:		

ODELL EDUCATION

DELINEATING ARGUMENTS: CASE STUDY

Baseball Sharks

ISSUE

It is winter and the parents of an eighth-grader named Jesse are trying to help him determine which baseball team he should play for in the upcoming spring and summer. Jesse is already a fantastic shortstop and pitcher who is being told by his coach that he is better than most high school players. He wants to play with a good team that challenges him but he hates all the travel required by the teams that are really good. Matt is the coach of the best team in the region, the Sharks. The Sharks will travel every weekend from April–July to play in tournaments. Most of these trips are two to three hours or more away. These tournaments are played at colleges and universities and give college coaches and even Major League scouts the opportunity to watch these young athletes compete.

Many of these players are then recruited throughout high school by Major League teams and colleges. Jesse's parents are trying to help him make the best decision and will support him whatever he decides.

Matt, the Shark's coach, is coming over to speak with Jesse and his parents about playing with the Sharks. Jesse's parents are supportive of him and want him to make the best decision for himself.

PERSPECTIVES

COACH MATT

Matt is the Sharks' coach and really wants Jesse to play for him this summer. Matt sees Jesse as a vital piece to his team's success. There are other shortstops that could play for him but none come close to having the skill set Jesse owns. Matt also believes Jesse can play baseball collegiately and if he continues to get the right type of exposure, he could be drafted into the Major Leagues during high school.

He presents the following argument:

Playing for the Sharks will give you the exposure you need to get an athletic scholarship for college and could lead to you being drafted into Major League Baseball.

Between April and July Jesse will be seen and evaluated by college coaches and Major League scouts. Each tournament provides college coaches and professional scouts access to the best players in the country and enables them to evaluate many players at one time. This access to the decision makers at the next level of competition should be highly valued to someone like Jesse.

The travel schedule is time intensive but a modest price to pay for the opportunities playing collegiate baseball and perhaps professional baseball could provide. We travel a lot. This is because we want our players to have the best possible opportunity to be seen by a variety of coaches from different colleges and universities and be seen by as many professional scouts as possible. It's a sacrifice of time now, but a college scholarship or Major League signing bonus provides a lot of opportunity.

The competition you will face on a nightly basis while playing for the Sharks is incomparable and will make you a better player. Our schedule is demanding and is created to compete against the best teams in the region and the country.

In conclusion, if Jesse wants to play college baseball and be considered professionally, his best chance is to play with the Sharks.

JESSE'S PARENTS

Jesse's parents want to help him make the best decision. They recognize the dilemma he faces and understand the pros and cons of both sides. They feel that Matt is pressuring Jesse to join the Sharks and know the opportunities that playing with them could open up, but they do not want Jesse to make a decision out of pressure or fear.

Baseball Sharks (Continued)

Jesse's parents present the following argument:

Although the Sharks definitely would provide Jesse the best opportunity to pursue a future baseball career, he may not be ready to make this decision. Jesse is an eighth-grader and has several more years before he must decide where he wants to attend school.

Jesse is not ready to commit his entire summer to one activity. Although baseball is important to Jesse, we recognize that being well rounded requires participating in multiple activities and we believe he should get to pursue those that he wants to. Playing on the Sharks would mean he'd have less time at the beach where he loves to swim.

The local team will enable Jesse to continue playing baseball, work on his skills, and not spend all his time on the road. We know the quality and access the local team can provide Jesse are not as good as the Sharks. They're not bad though.

He has been able to develop to this point. And his friend Luke is on the team as well. Playing for the hometown team means he gets to continue playing baseball as well as spend time with his friends.

In conclusion, we want Jesse to have all the information necessary to make the best decision for himself. Although he does want to play baseball collegiately and have the chance to be drafted into Major League Baseball, he is not ready to commit himself completely to just baseball. We want to help Jesse think through both sides of the decision and then support whatever he decides.

OTHER PERSPECTIVES

Jesse, Jesse's older brother, Luke, Jesse's friend

Topic Baseball Sharks—Coach Matt

ISSUE	Eighth-grader Jesse is an excellent baseball player with potential to play in college and the pros. The coach of a highly competitive team wants him to play this summer. Playing on the team would be an incredible opportunity to develop his skills and to play in front of college and pro scouts. The travel required by the team, however, would mean that playing baseball would be just about all he did this summer. He can always play for a less competitive local team that would allow him more time for other activities.
PERSPECTIVE	Matt is the coach of the Sharks. He sees Jesse as a potential key player on his team. He also sees that playing for the Sharks would be good for Jesse's skills and exposure.
POSITION	Jesse should play on the Sharks this summer.

CLAIM 1	CLAIM 2	CLAIM 3
Playing for the Sharks will give Jesse the exposure he needs to get an athletic scholarship for college and could lead to being drafted into Major League Baseball.	The travel schedule is time intensive but a modest price to pay for the opportunities playing collegiate baseball and perhaps professional baseball could provide.	The competition you will face on a nightly basis while playing for the Sharks is incomparable and will make you a better player.
Supporting evidence:	**Supporting evidence:**	**Supporting evidence:**
College and Major League scouts attend the tournaments that the Sharks play.	The intensive travel is because the coach wants the players to play with the best teams around the area at their level. It's a sacrifice of time now, but a college scholarship or Major League signing bonus provides a lot of opportunity.	Our schedule is demanding and is created to compete against the best teams in the region and the country.

Name Model

Topic Baseball Sharks—Jesse's Parents

ISSUE	Eighth-grader Jesse is an excellent baseball player with potential to play in college and the pros. The coach of a highly competitive team wants him to play this summer. Playing on the team would be an incredible opportunity to develop his skills and to play in front of college and pro scouts. The travel required by the team, however, would mean that playing baseball would be just about all he did this summer. He can instead play for a less competitive local team that would allow him more time for other activities.
PERSPECTIVE	Jesse's parents support him in everything he does. They recognize he has a gift for baseball and that playing it is and will be important in his life. They also want him to experience many things including just plain enjoying himself. They feel that Jesse is feeling some pressure—especially because the coach is so interested in him. They want him to make the decision without feeling any pressure.
POSITION	Jesse should not play on the Sharks this summer.

CLAIM 1	**CLAIM 2**	**CLAIM 3**
Jesse is too young to commit so much time to one activity.	Although the Sharks are better, the hometown team will still give him opportunity to play baseball.	Not playing with the Sharks will give him more time with his friends.
Supporting evidence:	**Supporting evidence:**	**Supporting evidence:**
He has other interests that would suffer from spending so much time playing baseball. He would spend less time swimming at the beach.	He's not giving up playing baseball. So far his experience with the hometown team has been good.	He'll spend less time on the road. And his friend Luke plays on the hometown team, too.

ODELL EDUCATION

DELINEATING ARGUMENTS: CASE STUDY

Friending a Teacher

Mr. Higgins is a twenty-three-year-old Social Studies teacher at Thunder Ridge Middle School. Over the weekend, he received a friend request on Facebook from Derek, who is one of his students. Derek is a B student who is generally quiet in class. Mr. Higgins has never had a problem with Derek, but he also hasn't interacted with Derek much, either inside or out of class. In order to keep his school life separate from his personal life, Mr. Higgins decided when he took the job at Thunder Ridge that he would not accept a friend request from any of his students. When Derek's parents hear that Mr. Higgins did not accept Derek's request, they schedule a meeting with Mr. Higgins to demand that he accept the request. They are worried that Mr. Higgins will damage Derek's confidence in school if he continues to reject their son's request.

DEREK

Derek considers himself a technically savvy student. He thinks that social media are fascinating and he is an avid user of Facebook. One of the reasons he likes Facebook is that it gives teachers and students a way to get to know one another outside of class. Derek sent the request to Mr. Higgins in order to include Facebook as part of the learning environment at Thunder Ridge.

At the meeting, Derek explains why he thinks Mr. Higgins should accept his request:

Look, Mr. Higgins. Everyone is on Facebook these days. You should know this because you have a profile and even with your privacy settings I can tell you use it a lot. If you are using Facebook, you should be a good Facebook citizen and accept requests from people. It's just part of the deal. And it's not a big deal. There's no harm in being friends with students. If you post something, you're okay sharing it, so why not let me learn a bit more about you? I mean, I'll find out anyway when I Google you, so it's not like there are a lot of secrets to find. What really makes me mad about rejecting my friend request is that you aren't treating me fairly. I never do anything wrong in class, so there is no reason to reject my request.

MR. HIGGINS

Mr. Higgins is a popular teacher at Thunder Ridge. He is well known for creating new ways to bring technology to the classroom. Most of the students at Thunder Ridge follow him on Twitter. He doesn't hold Derek's request against him, but Mr. Higgins decided before he started his job that accepting friend requests from any student wouldn't be a good idea.

Mr. Higgins explains his decision to Derek:

Even though online platforms are changing the way students and teachers interact, there need to be boundaries. Facebook is a personal space and if I accept your request, I am worried that you'll forget that I am your teacher. There is a further problem to keep in mind. If I accept your request, I am obligated to accept a request from any student. Even if I had a guarantee that you would handle being friends on Facebook appropriately, I cannot be sure about this with everyone, so I don't want to be in a position in which others can accuse me of playing favorites based on what friend requests I accept. And I'd like to ask you, Derek, if you are friends with your parents on Facebook? I'm guessing that you are probably like most of your classmates who don't want to be friends with their parents because they want to keep their social lives private. My Facebook account is no different. It is a place for me to have a life that is separate from my job as your teacher.

OTHER PERSPECTIVES

Derek's parents, Derek's classmates, Mr. Higgins's colleagues

DELINEATING ARGUMENTS: CASE STUDY

Tweeting about a Pop Quiz

ISSUE

Justin has Spanish class during first period. When the bell rings Monday morning, the teacher announces that there will be a pop quiz. Justin studied over the weekend, so he's confident he did well on the quiz. His friend Mark, however, told Justin on the ride to school that he didn't study at all. Mark has Spanish with the same teacher during third period. Justin decides to Tweet a warning to Mark about the pop quiz so that Mark will have second period to study. Mark sees the Tweet and he studies during his history class.

His grade on the pop quiz is much higher than his average grade for the course, so the teacher becomes suspicious. The teacher eventually finds out that Justin Tweeted a warning to Mark about the quiz. The teacher calls a meeting with Justin and the school principal to inform Justin that the Tweet was cheating and he will be penalized as such. Justin argues that the Tweet isn't cheating and he shouldn't be punished for letting Mark know about the quiz.

PERSPECTIVES

THE TEACHER

The teacher has been at the school for more than twenty years. During that time, she has earned a reputation as a hard but fair grader. She has been nominated for teacher of the year several times. She has a policy in her class that cell phones are not allowed to be on.

The teacher explains why she considers the Tweet to be cheating:

When I decide to give a pop quiz, I want to evaluate whether my students are keeping up with the ideas and homework in my course. These quizzes need to be surprises in order to evaluate students' commitment to my course. I don't announce these quizzes ahead of time because this will just encourage students to study at the last minute. This doesn't provide the insight I want into students' performance. Because Justin sent that message to his friend, there was an opportunity for his friend and anyone else who heard about this message to prepare for the quiz. This is an unfair advantage and the grades for the third-period quizzes will almost certainly be higher. This isn't fair to my first-period students. In addition to undermining my quiz, Justin has also created extra work for me. I'll have to redo the quiz at another surprise point in the course. I am going to have to deal with complaints from students who did well on the quiz but will have to take a replacement.

JUSTIN

Justin is a good student. His GPA is a 3.7 and he takes a couple of AP courses. He is also involved in the speech and debate team and the chess club. He glazes hams for extra money on the weekend. He and Mark have been friends for five years, though they aren't best friends. Mark moved to Justin's treet so they often see one another over the weekend. Justin knows that Mark struggles with school.

Justin defends his decision to Tweet with the following statement:

Sending a Tweet isn't cheating because I didn't tell Mark or anyone else who saw the Tweet what was on the quiz. I just said that we had a quiz so they might have a quiz. I had no idea if the teacher was going to have a quiz for the third-period class. I can't read her mind. What I did isn't different from the other students who told their friends about the quiz in person. Besides, couldn't Mark have thought there might be a quiz even if he hadn't seen the Tweet? At the end of the day, Mark studied and did well, so I don't see what the problem is. It doesn't matter what I Tweeted or what he thought. What matters is that he spent time preparing for the quiz and he earned his grade.

OTHER PERSPECTIVES

Other students, the principal, the teacher's colleagues

ODELL
EDUCATION

NOTES

Developing Core Literacy Proficiencies

Developing Core Literacy Proficiencies

Developing Core Literacy Proficiencies

....

....

....

....

....

....

....

....

....

....

....

....

....

....

....

....

....

....

....

....

....

....

....

....

....

....

....

Developing Core Literacy Proficiencies

Developing Core Literacy Proficiencies

Developing Core Literacy Proficiencies